Rays –

STAND STRONG AS A

MIGHTY MAN OF GOD!

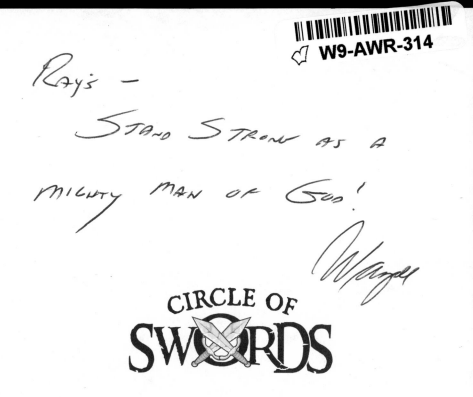

CIRCLE OF
SWORDS

CIRCLE OF SWORDS

Becoming a Mighty Man of God

WAYDE WILSON

WESTBOW®
PRESS
A DIVISION OF THOMAS NELSON
& ZONDERVAN

cover design and interior graphics by Wayne Wilson

Unless otherwise identified, Scripture quotations are from the HOLY BIBLE, NEW INTERNATIONAL VERSION®, NIV® Copyright © 1973, 1978, 1984, 2011 by Biblica. Used by permission. All rights reserved worldwide. Scripture quotations marked NLT are from the Holy Bible, New Living Translation, copyright © 1996, 2004, 2007 by Tyndale House Foundation. Used by permission of Tyndale House Publishers, Inc., Carol Stream, Illinois 60188. All rights reserved. Scripture quotations marked MSG are taken from The Message. Copyright © 1993, 1994, 1995, 1996, 2000, 2001, 2002. Used by permission of NavPress Publishing Group. Scripture quotations marked NCV are from the New Century Version®. Copyright © 2005 by Thomas Nelson, Inc. Used by permission. All rights reserved. Scripture quotations marked ERV are from the Easy-to-Read Version. Copyright © 2006 by World Bible Translation Center. Emphasis within Scripture is the author's own.

WestBow Press books may be ordered through booksellers or by contacting:

WestBow Press
A Division of Thomas Nelson & Zondervan
1663 Liberty Drive
Bloomington, IN 47403
www.westbowpress.com
1 (866) 928-1240

Because of the dynamic nature of the Internet, any web addresses or links contained in this book may have changed since publication and may no longer be valid. The views expressed in this work are solely those of the author and do not necessarily reflect the views of the publisher, and the publisher hereby disclaims any responsibility for them.

Any people depicted in stock imagery provided by Thinkstock are models, and such images are being used for illustrative purposes only. Certain stock imagery © Thinkstock.

ISBN: 978-1-4908-5395-6 (sc)
ISBN: 978-1-4908-5393-2 (hc)
ISBN: 978-1-4908-5394-9 (e)

Library of Congress Control Number: 2014917622

Print information available on the last page.

WestBow Press rev. date: 4/10/2015

DEDICATION

To the beautiful women in my life—my amazing wife, Sonya, and my daughter, Tristin, who believed this book should be written and bugged me until it finally was. Thanks for loving and believing in me.

To my sons Trevor and Travis—my greatest prayer is that you will become mighty men of God.

A man is not great because he is popular, or rich because he has a lot of money; true greatness comes from knowing God. And the man who is respected in his own home and loved by his family is richest of all.

ENDORSEMENTS

Wayde Wilson inspires men to get excited about the Word of God through the story of David and his mighty men. In *Circle of Swords* you will be encouraged to pursue God with all your heart, and armed with tools for gaining courage, integrity, and confidence to become the man, husband, father, friend, and leader God is calling you to be.

Wilfredo "Choco" De Jesús, Senior Pastor
New Life Covenant Church, Chicago, Illinois
Author, *Amazing Faith* and *In the Gap*

Wayde Wilson speaks "Man." Each chapter confronts issues that every man faces with practical solutions straight from the manliest portions of God's Word. *Circle of Swords* is fast-moving, fun-reading, in-your-face-challenging, and life-changing! Excellent for small groups or individual growth.

Tim Enloe
Author and Conference Speaker

I not only recommend *Circle of Swords*, but I commend the author of this book. He has lived the life that gives him the authority to teach the principles on these pages. I have known Wayde from his early teen years. His faithful commitment to the pursuit of godly manhood is an endorsement within itself. Every paragraph is not only biblically sound, but validated by the writer's personal experience.

Tom Greene
Greene & Raley Ministry
Advancement Group

Wayde Wilson is the William Wallace of our generation, challenging men to grab their swords and let the adventure begin! His book is a game changer for you and your band of brothers. *Circle of Swords* will inspire you to put down your remote control and do something heroic for God!

Tom Rees
HonorBound Men's Director
PennDel Ministry Network

CONTENTS

PREFACE

Circle of Swords honors the memory of my friend, Chris Seiff. In the fall of 2012, Chris, Hector Hoyos, and Mike Blattenberger joined me on a 21-week discipleship journey. It was one of the greatest adventures I've ever been part of. Four strangers became life-long friends and I watched Chris, Mike, and Hector become men of God.

On February 1, 2014, when I was about halfway done writing this book, Chris's life tragically ended. He was just beginning to tap into his vast God-given potential. Every time someone tells me this book inspired him to be a man of God, I will think of Chris.

This book was written at a time in my life when I felt lonely, isolated, forgotten, unimportant, and uncertain of my future. But, like David, I *"found strength in the Lord my God."*[1] One day during a time of prayer, when I was close to completing the book, I remember thinking, *God often used people who felt broken and unworthy to do great things...and His greatness is best displayed in and through our weakness.*

At that moment, I prayed, "God, I give this book to You. Use it to impact the lives of men."

The book you hold in your hands that now belongs to you, first belonged to God. I pray He will use it uniquely in your life and that the Holy Spirit will supernaturally empower the words and ideas you read to help challenge and change you into the man God always knew you could be.

INTRODUCTION

This book is for guys. Guys who like action movies over chick-flicks. Guys who would rather read comic books, *Field & Stream, Sports Illustrated,* or *Hot Rod* magazines instead of long, boring novels with no pictures. Guys who grill meat, watch sports, ride Harleys, play practical jokes, and sit around campfires with their buddies laughing and telling crazy stories. *And,* it's for guys who get about as excited over the idea of a Bible Study or Support Group as they do an afternoon shopping at the mall.

Here's the thing: the Bible is an awesome book full of great advice that can help you live a better life and learn how to know God. But lots of men don't read the Bible, and they don't know how to relate to God or to guys who do.

So, I wrote this book for *that guy*. Am I crazy? Yes I am. And I have a lot of crazy guys I call friends. When we get together to hunt, fish, or watch a game, we have a great time. We laugh...A LOT. We live for adventure. We try to out-do each other. (It's a guy thing.) But behind all that testosterone-infused chest-thumping, we're just grown-up boys in men's bodies. We need what every human being needs: acceptance, friendship, encouragement—and a relationship with God. *We just don't like to talk about those things.* And we sure don't like when the conversation gets all mushy (emotional). I get it. I'm a guy.

But I also know that deep inside, every man wants to make a difference; to live a life of adventure; to be respected and admired;

to be someone's hero. So I'm pumped to introduce you to a group of guys in the Bible you're going to totally relate to. Chances are, you've never even *heard* of them or won't believe a group of guys this wild and crazy are even mentioned in God's Book. But they are! Many of them were outlaws when they met—armed and dangerous. They had a secret hideout in a cave! Their leader was a fugitive—WANTED: DEAD OR ALIVE. But guess what? *God loves fugitives and outlaws!* And through the influence of a godly leader, God turned a bunch of criminals into an elite group of commandos willing to lay down their lives for what—and Who—they believed in.

The Bible calls them *David's Mighty Men.* Thirty-seven of the baddest dudes in the Bible; the Green Berets of David's army. Check out this description of them:

> *They were brave warriors, ready for battle and able to handle the shield and spear. **Their faces were the faces of lions.**... Day after day [such] men came to help David, until he had a great army, like the army of God.*[1]

If you want to meet these guys and hear some of the crazy things they did, keep reading. Here's my promise to you to help you stay tuned:

- Short chapters
- Lots of guy stuff you will relate to
- In-Your-Face Challenges in each chapter
- You'll be a better man if you apply the things you read in your life

So whad'ya say...are you man enough to hang out with David's Mighty Men? Then grab your sword and let the adventure begin.

The Circle of Swords

There's no biblical evidence to prove it, but knowing guys like I do, I guarantee you David and his elite team of commandos had their own unique rallying cry—like a football team about to take the field or soldiers headed off to battle. At the end of meetings or before they would march out to war, I can see David and his thirty-seven Mighty Men forming a *Circle of Swords*. David and his top three leaders would step *into the middle* of the circle. Then, one at a time, each of the four leaders would shout a phrase, lifting his sword as he shouted. Each phrase was then repeated by the men in the outer circle as they raised and lowered their swords. It went like this:

David shouts, "To HONOR!" Men reply, "To HONOR!"

Second Leader, "To COURAGE!" Men, "To COURAGE!"

Third Leader, "To COMMITMENT!" Men, "To COMMITMENT!"

Fourth Leader, "To GOD!" Men, "To GOD!"

At some point, his men added, "To GOD and to DAVID!" at the end as their way of showing loyalty to their leader. The *Circle of Swords* inspired and unified David's Mighty Men and his army by constantly reminding them of what—and Who—they were fighting for. It also symbolized the commitment of David's men to their leader.

At the end of each chapter, I challenge you to put your sword in the circle, signifying you're all in on the theme that was just placed in front of you; committed to God as your leader. And I want you to remember as you go through life that you're not alone *unless you choose to be*. You are meant to belong to a band of brothers who fight for what is right and have each other's backs as elite members

of the *Circle of Swords:* "To Honor, To Courage, To Commitment...
To God!"

The Challenge: To Become a Mighty Man of God

Only thirty-seven bad-to-the-bone guys made it onto David's list of
Mighty Men. They didn't become part of this elite group of warriors
by being average. They proved themselves on the field of battle again
and again.

Do you want to be average, or do you want to be a Mighty Man of
God?

If you want to be average, you can stop reading now. This book isn't
for you. You're content to play it safe, never take risks, compromise,
waste valuable opportunities, make excuses, and in general, refuse
to discover and live up to your God-given potential. Too many men
settle for being average. Don't be one of them!

If you want to be a Mighty Man of God, then don't just read this
book—*accept the challenge to become a better man!* A man who is
committed to his family and friends. A man who is trustworthy,
unwilling to compromise or make excuses. A man who is ready
to take on challenges and fight for what's right. If you want to be
respected and live up to your God-given potential, then you've got
to be willing to step onto the battlefield and fight!

Here are the tools you'll need to come out on the other side of this
book a Mighty Man of God:

- A *determined attitude* driven by simple, honest prayers and a
  willingness to give God a chance to speak to you and change
  you. Here's an example of a prayer you could pray before you

read a chapter, *"God, I want You to use what I'm about to read to speak to me, challenge me, and make me a better man. Thanks for Your help! Amen."*

- A *commitment* to read and respond to each chapter.
- A *Bible* in a translation that makes sense to you; in printed or digital form. The FREE *YouVersion* Bible App lets you take the Bible with you on your phone or tablet wherever you go! If you're not sure which translation to use, try the New Living Translation.
- A *pen or pencil* to write notes and answer the In-Your-Face Challenges.

Advanced Training: If you want to take it up a notch and go Green Beret, add the following to your training routine:

- *Go Mano-a-Mano.* Proverbs 27:17 says, *"As iron sharpens iron, so one person sharpens another."* Find another guy who's serious about wanting to be a Mighty Man of God and get together once a week to talk about what you read. Push each other by asking hard questions, praying for each other, and holding one another accountable.
- Sharpen your sword by *memorizing the Word.* Bible verses inspire us, challenge us, and remind us of what's important. I've included theme verses at the end of each chapter. Even if you only memorize one or two them, that's one or two more verses than you had memorized when you started! Psalm 119:11 says it well, *"I have hidden your word in my heart, that I might not sin against you."*

Form your own Circle of Swords! Purchase the Circle of Swords Small Group Leader's Guide, at www.waydewilson.com

———◈———

David: Man among Mighty Men

David is one of my favorite Bible characters. Here are some of the reasons why, as a man, I can *relate* to David (and why I believe you will too):

David was a "man's man."

David was *a rugged outdoorsman.* As a shepherd, David learned *survival skills* for keeping himself and his father's sheep alive out in the wilderness. He slept under the stars to the sound of jackals howling in the night. He worked in the hot desert sun among snakes and scorpions with the wind and sand in his face.[2] He knew how to find food, water, shelter, and start a fire. David and Bear Grylls would have gotten along great.[3]

He was *a skilled soldier and weapons expert.* David was expertly self-trained in hand-to-hand combat with knives, swords, and spears. He would have enjoyed watching "Deadliest Warriors."[4] He could shoot a bow and arrow and he was deadly with a slingshot. I'm not just talking birds and rabbits; he killed a lion, a bear, and the giant Philistine champion, Goliath, with a sling! (I have trouble hitting a target with a modern wrist-rocket slingshot!) David could have held his own with any of the competitors on "Top Shot."[5]

He was *a leader of men.* Men of all kinds were drawn to David. He had the ability to take both the elite of society as well as outlaws and rejects, challenge them up, and make them better men. Guys wanted to hang out with him, to be in his inner circle. He was respected and admired. He was cool. He was tough. Women loved him. Men wanted to be like him. (Think Brad Pitt or Clint Eastwood.) And yet, in spite of the fact that he was a "man's man"...

David wasn't afraid to "get real."

Lots of men are afraid to show their emotions. Not David. He was *a musician and poet*. The same guy who was a rugged outdoorsman, soldier, and respected leader of men, wrote deeply personal poems and songs and sang them as he accompanied himself on the harp (think of it as his version of the electric or acoustic guitar). No wonder the chicks loved him! He was good looking[6] and he had a string of "greatest hits" that are still popular today.[7] And...

He was *spiritually and relationally honest*. Whatever emotion he was feeling—fear, anger, disappointment, loneliness, love, joy, sadness, guilt—David wasn't afraid to put it all out there with his words and songs. As an outdoorsman, musician, and writer myself, I appreciate David's example of a tough guy who wasn't afraid to show his emotions. There's another reason I relate to David:

David was an underdog.

When we meet David in 1 Samuel 16, God has rejected Saul as king of Israel. God tells Samuel the prophet to go to the house of Jesse because, *"I have chosen one of his sons to be king."*[8] When he arrives, Samuel asks Jesse to introduce him to his sons. Samuel is so impressed when he sees Eliab, the oldest, that he instantly thinks, *Surely the Lord's anointed stands here.* But he was wrong. Eliab wasn't God's choice. Neither were any of the next six brothers.

One by one, Samuel evaluated seven top draft choices and God didn't pick *any* of them. Samuel asks, "Are these all the sons you have?" Jesse says, "There's one more...the youngest. But he's out with the sheep." Translation: "He's just a boy. Why bother?" They send for David and when he arrives, God says, *"That's My man. Anoint him; he's the one."*[9] And David, the little guy, the runt of the litter, the youngest of eight brothers, is anointed as the next king of Israel!

He was overlooked by everyone...*but God*. David learned something about God that day, and because of David's story, so do we. Here it is:

> *The Lord does not look at the things people look at. People look at the outward appearance, but* **the Lord looks at the heart** (1 Samuel 16:7).

God is for the underdog. God sees things in us that others miss. His evaluation doesn't just go skin-deep—it goes *heart*-deep. When others saw a shepherd boy, God could see a king. The *last* and the *least likely* was picked by God to be a great leader. It was a lesson David never forgot. Those are some of the reasons why, as a man, I can *relate* to David. Now let's talk about what made him *a great leader*.

FOLLOW THE LEADER

Many people joined David. There were men who were in some kind of trouble, men who owed a lot of money, and men who were just not satisfied with life...and he became their leader. He had about 400 men with him.

1 Samuel 22:2 (ERV)

Day after day men came to help David, until he had a great and mighty army, like the army of God.

1 Chronicles 12:22 (NIV)

Big Idea: Who you follow determines your destiny.

Characteristics of a Great Leader

"Leadership is influence." –John Maxwell

Who are the influencers in your life? Is their influence having a positive or negative impact on you? Great leaders inspire us to do great things and be better people.

List some examples of great leaders and what makes them great.

Leader   What made/makes this person great?

_____   _____

_____   _____

_____   _____

_____   _____

David's leadership turned outlaws into heroes and influenced men headed for trouble to become Mighty Men of God. Let's look at five characteristics that made David a great leader.

1. David had a heart for God. When you evaluate David as a leader, you have to start here. You won't find it listed in many books on the subject, but everything about *David's leadership* was influenced by this characteristic. David, like few men who have ever lived, had a deep desire to honor God. He also had a uniquely close and personal relationship with God. And this relationship earned David a one-of-a-kind description given to him by God himself: *a man after God's own heart.*

> *After removing Saul,* [God] *made David...king. God testified concerning him: "I have found David son of Jesse, **a man after my own heart...**"*[1]

I used to think the description "a man after God's own heart" meant David was a man with a heart *like* God's. But that's not accurate because, in addition to his many great qualities, David had flaws and sins—*big ones.* The Bible doesn't hide David's failures. Here's a list of his worst: adulterer, liar, betrayer, and murderer. That's heavy stuff. God isn't an adulterer or a liar or a murderer, so the description cannot mean David had a heart *like* God's.

The key to understanding God's description of David is found in the word *after*. One of the definitions for *after* is "in pursuit of," as in, "I looked back and a bear was comin' *after* me!" That means a bear was chasing you. That's a good way to describe David. He wasn't a perfect man, but he was a man *in constant pursuit of* God. When David fell, he fell hard. But when he got up, David never stopped chasing God. I hope you're encouraged by the fact that even though he was flawed, David was still known as "a man after God's own heart." That means *there's hope for us!*

In the same verse (Acts 13:22), God says, "...[David] *will do everything I want him to do."* Because David never stopped pursuing God, even when he sinned and failed, he was still able to accomplish everything God wanted him to do as a leader. In fact, Acts 13:36 makes a powerful statement about David's life: *"David served God's purpose in his own generation."* What a way to be remembered! Even with his flaws, David served the purpose for which he was born. And the outlaws and outcasts who followed him as he pursued God not only shared in his success, but David showed them how to become God chasers too.

2. David was sold out. The phrase "all in" is popular right now. It's a way of saying a person is *completely committed to something or someone.* That was David. When David made a commitment, he was all in. He didn't want to just be an average shepherd, musician, friend, soldier, or leader; he wanted to be the best he could be.[2] First Samuel 18:5 says, *"Whatever [King] Saul sent him to do, David did it so successfully that Saul gave him a high rank in the army."* Sold out for David was more than a *commitment to excellence;* it was also *a no-quit attitude.* If David believed in something, no way was he backing down. He was willing to lay it all on the line. David's sold-out attitude made him a great leader and resulted in followers who were willing to lay down their lives for him.

3. David had courage. Every time I read the story of David and Goliath[3] I get pumped up by David's courage. The Israelites were at war with their most-hated enemies, the Philistines. The Philistine army was camped on one hill, and the Israeli army was camped on an opposite hill, with a valley between them. Every day the Philistine champion, a giant of a man named Goliath, would walk out into the valley, curse the Israelites, mock God, and challenge King Saul to send his best man to fight him in a winner-takes-all battle. If Goliath won, the Israelites would become the Philistine's slaves. If someone could defeat him, the Philistines would become slaves to the Israelites.

The Bible says Goliath was so intimidating that, *"When Saul* [who by the way "stood a head taller than anyone else in Israel" [4]] *and his troops heard the Philistine's challenge, **they were terrified and lost all hope**."*[5] King Saul and his men were shaking in their sandals. Can you blame them? Goliath was over *nine feet tall,* wore *125 pounds of armor,* and the head of his spear weighed over *15 pounds!*[6] Goliath was a bad man—a state-of-the-art soldier. Seemingly indestructible. Until David showed up. His dad sent him to deliver cheese sandwiches to his three older brothers who were soldiers in Saul's army.[7] While David was having lunch with his brothers, Goliath stepped onto the battlefield and started mouthing off, cussing and mocking God— challenging someone to come out and fight him.

David's response is awesome: *"Who is this uncircumcised Philistine that he should defy the armies of the living God?"*[8] All the big, tough, trained soldiers were freaking out, but the sandwich delivery boy was ready to fight: "Are you guys gonna sit back and let this big jerk talk like that about our God?! *Let me at him!"* And in one of the most famous battles in history, little David with his big faith in God took down the giant. David's conversation with Goliath is too good to miss. Imagine watching this scene on a movie screen set to some epic theme music:

*...with nothing but a sling in his hand, David approached the Philistine champion. Seeing that he was just a boy, Goliath **despised him** shouting, "Am I a dog that you come at me with sticks?" And he cursed David by his gods. "Come here, boy! And I'll give your flesh to the birds!"*

*Standing his ground, David answered, "You come against me with sword and spear and javelin, but I come against you **in the name of the Lord Almighty**, the God of the armies of Israel you have defied. Today the Lord will hand you over to me. I'll strike you down and cut off your head...and the whole world will know that **there is a God in Israel!"***

Enraged, Goliath roared and attacked. As David ran to meet him, he reached in his bag, took out a stone, slipped it into his sling, and with a flick of his wrist, launched it; striking the giant between the eyes. With a solid thud, the stone sank deep into Goliath's forehead and he fell, first to his knees, then facedown on the ground. David ran, stood over Goliath, drew the giant's sword from its sheath and thrust it into the Philistine's chest. Then he cut off Goliath's head and held it up for everyone to see.

*When they saw that their champion was dead, the Philistines ran for their lives. So David triumphed over the Philistine with just a sling and a stone. His words that day were never forgotten, "It is not by sword or spear that the Lord saves; **for the battle is the Lord's!"**[9]*

Man that's gutsy! I want to be like David! Who wouldn't want to follow a leader with that kind of courage!? David knew deep in his heart that if God was with him, he couldn't lose! And it made him a fearless leader who inspired courage in others.

4. David had integrity. Integrity is doing what's right when no one is watching and everyone else is compromising. Up until his sin with Bathsheba, David was a living example of that definition. He did what was right, even when it was hard and he had opportunities to cut corners. You might be thinking, *David's been anointed to be the next king of Israel. He's a hero after defeating Goliath. He's on his way to the top!* Well, he was...sort of. But David's road to the throne was a lot longer and harder than he would have ever imagined. So hard in fact, that there were many days when David wondered *how,* or *if* he would ever become king.[10] Let me give you a brief summary:[11]

Because God was with him, David quickly moved up through the ranks and became a leader in Saul's army. He was invited to live in the king's palace. David and Saul's son, Jonathan, became best friends. Saul's daughter, Michal, fell in love with and married David. He was respected by his peers and loved by the people. Everything was great until one day, as King Saul and his troops were returning from battle, all the women from the surrounding towns came out dancing and singing this little song: "Saul has slain his thousands, and David *his tens of thousands.*"[12]

That moment was a game changer for David. The Bible says, *"Saul was very angry... [when he heard the song]. And from that time on Saul kept a close [jealous] eye on David."*[13] Jealousy took over Saul's life. He became a madman obsessed with killing David—even though David was completely loyal to him. David eventually had to run for his life. Saul put a bounty on his head. The hero became an outlaw: Wanted: Dead or Alive. David went from living in the king's palace to hiding out in the desert, sleeping in caves.

It was a tough time for David. And yet it was during those difficult years when he was running from Saul that God shaped David into a great leader. *Anyone can lead in the good times; but a true leader is someone who can inspire people in tough times.* Before long an army began to form around David; nearly four hundred men including his brothers and family, and a bunch of outlaws, rejects, and guys who were down on their luck.

Think about it: David was the leader of an *army* of *outlaws.* He could have taken the kingdom by force; become like Billy the Kid or Jesse James, and terrorized the country. There *is* no law when you're an *outlaw!* Instead, *twice* David had the opportunity to kill Saul,[14] but he refused to take power that way and spared Saul's life saying, *"The Lord forbid that I should do such a thing to my master, the Lord's anointed."*[15] Think how hard that would have been! But by his example, David's men saw a leader who trusted God when it didn't make sense and when it would have been easy and justifiable to take matters into his own hands. David showed outlaws how to live with integrity! He did the right thing even when it was hard. His men respected him for it. And God honored him for it.

5. David stood up for the underdog. Have you ever been the last guy picked for the team? It's a lousy feeling. Most guys can remember a scene like this: The neighborhood gang gathered for a game of football (tackle for tough guys; two-hand touch for wimps). Two captains took turns choosing teammates one at a time. The popular, athletic guys always got picked first and the selection process continued until there was *that one guy* left. You know who I'm talking about; the uncoordinated guy with the thick glasses. You probably still remember his name. He went to the team who had no choice. No one ever threw him the ball. He might as well have been invisible except to the guys on the other team who smacked him around.

David knew what it felt like to be *that guy*. Remember? Last of eight brothers. Runt of the litter. The sandwich delivery boy. But God picked David when everyone else looked past him. And David never forgot it. So David built an army of underdogs. The unwanted. The imperfect. The misunderstood. The failures. The rejects of society. *"Men who were in some kind of trouble, men who owed a lot of money, and men who were just not satisfied with life."*[16] Bad, broke, and bored! The guys no one else wanted became David's army. No wait...they became something more: *"Day after day men* [underdogs] *came to help David, until he had a great and mighty army, like the army of God."*[17] That's AWESOME! David's godly leadership transformed *rejects* into *heroes*. The guys no one else wanted became God's First Team; from *outlaws* to *warriors* in the army of God!

Who Are You Following?

Can you hear God speaking to you? He's saying, *"I want you. I believe in you. I have a mission for you. And I'm calling you to serve Me like a man!"*

The BIG IDEA for this chapter is *who you follow determines your destiny*. A lot of men who could do great things in the world are headed nowhere—or for disaster—because they're *not following the right leader*. Or because *they* are trying to *be* the leader, but they have no idea *how to do it* or *where they're going*. So let me get in your face with some important questions.

In-Your-Face Challenge:

What leader(s) are you following?

Are they making you a better man? _____ YES _____ NO

Husband? _____ YES _____ NO

Father? _____ YES _____ NO

How many of the characteristics that made David a great leader do they have?

_____ Heart for God

_____ Sold out (to a good cause)

_____ Courage

_____ Integrity

_____ Believe in the underdog (looks out for the overlooked)

_____ Other? Can you name *any* positive characteristic about the person(s) you're following?

If the leaders you're following are a negative influence, you need to make some tough but necessary decisions. Remember: *Today's decisions determine tomorrow's destinations.*

Follow THE Leader

Following the right leader changed the lives and destinies of criminals and outcasts, transforming them into David's Mighty Men. The Bible teaches that making Jesus Christ your Leader will change your life as well. You may not know much about Jesus. You may be thinking, *What qualifies him to be my leader?* If you research his life (and you should, don't just take my word for it), you'll find that Jesus had all the leadership characteristics David had...and more.

- Jesus Christ wasn't just a man with a heart *for* God; He *was and is* God. The Bible teaches that Jesus was God "in the flesh."[18] In other words, God in a man's body. And yet, even though He was God's Son, Jesus depended on God every day.[19]
- Jesus Christ was sold out for the cause. What was the cause? He came on a rescue mission to save us all from sin.[20] He was all in; giving His life for what He believed in.
- Jesus Christ was the most courageous man who has ever lived. David took on Goliath. Jesus took on Satan himself. What He did on the cross was the gutsiest thing anyone has ever done.[21]
- Jesus Christ didn't just have integrity; He was *perfect.* The Bible says Jesus was tempted in every way just like we are, but He never sinned.[22]
- Jesus Christ proved that God wants you! The Bible says, *"God **chose you**...to be saved."*[23] Another translation says it like this: *"God **picked you out** as his from the very start."*[24]

Like David, Jesus Christ wants guys like you and me who have "issues" to join His team.

Making Jesus Christ the Leader of your life is a big commitment. But if you go all in with Jesus, *He will change your life.* I want to say three things to you as you consider that decision:

First, it's *the most important decision* you will make in your life. The Bible teaches that where you spend eternity is determined by whether you accept or reject Jesus Christ.[25] You can make a bad decision that affects you for a day, a month, or even for the rest of your life; but you can't afford to be wrong about your eternity.

Second, God wants you to serve Him like a man. You don't have to turn in your "man card" to follow Jesus Christ! Like David, Jesus recruited real men to follow him.[26] Yes, you have to humble yourself to make Him your leader. But God isn't interested in recruiting men onto His team and then turning them into wimps. Throw out that idea and keep reading!

Third, go all in. Way too many men make halfhearted commitments to their wives, to their families—and to God. *Halfhearted commitments don't stick.* No one is forcing you to follow Jesus. It's your choice. But know this, Jesus gave *everything* for you on the cross. So don't make a halfhearted commitment to Him. Give Him your whole life!

When you're ready to make Jesus Christ *the* Leader of your life, turn to Appendix A for directions from the Bible on how to start a relationship with God.

*Following **the** Leader* is the first and most important step to becoming a Mighty Man of God. If more men would step up and follow Jesus Christ, together we could form *"a great and mighty army, like the*

11

army of God." And we could change the world. Are you ready to join the Circle of Swords?

To Honor, To Courage, To Commitment...To God!

Sharpen your sword by memorizing this verse: Jesus said, *"Whoever follows me will never live in darkness. They will have the light that gives life"* (John 8:12 ERV).

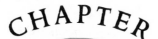

CHAPTER 2

WHAT'S IN A NAME?

These are the names of David's mighty men. There were thirty-seven in all.

2 SAMUEL 23:8, 39 (NIV)

It is better to be respected than to be rich. A good name is worth more than silver or gold.

PROVERBS 22:1 (ERV)

Big Idea: A man's name and his reputation are closely linked.

Hall of Fame Names

> *Standing in the hall of fame*
> *And the world's gonna know your name*
> *'Cause you burn with the brightest flame*
> *And you'll be on the walls of the hall of fame.*[1]

There are currently 280 members of the Pro Football Hall of Fame.[2] The list of inductees includes players, coaches, and contributors

13

(owners and team or league officials) who have "made outstanding contributions to professional football." Only the best-of-the-best get in. Think about it; out of thousands of guys who have played football at the elite college level, only a small percentage are talented enough to make it in the National Football League (NFL). And out of all the incredibly talented athletes who played in the NFL, only 251 have busts in Canton.[3] Most of their names are instantly recognizable, even to the marginal football fan. Names like Namath, Butkus, Dorsett, Montana, Staubach, and Unitas. Those are Hall of Fame names!

David's Mighty Men were *Hall of Famers*. The best-of-the best. Out of thousands of soldiers who served under David, only thirty-seven elite warriors made the cut. If you haven't read the list yet, take five minutes and check it out in 2 Samuel 23:8-39 and/or 1 Chronicles 11:10-47. Of David's thirty-seven Hall of Famers, five were so outstanding that they are mentioned separately, along with a brief description of their most famous acts of courage. They are: Josheb-Basshebeth (Jashobeam), Eleazar, and Shammah; David's top three officers. Abishai, commander over all of David's troops. And Benaiah, David's personal bodyguard.

Like Butkus, Unitas, and Namath, all you had to do was say these guy's names and everyone knew who you were talking about. Their names carried instant respect because they had proven themselves over and over again on the battlefield. But I remind you again that this elite group of Hall of Famers were part of that bunch of early recruits the Bible describes as *"Men who were in some kind of trouble, men who owed a lot of money, and men who were just not satisfied with life."*[4] Don't miss the point: Guys whose names once meant trouble or loser went down in history as Hall of Famers.

What's in a Name?

Every group of guys I've been part of—from sports teams to close friends—make up nicknames for each other. Nicknames are a sign of *belonging* and a *unique descriptive identification*.

Nicknames seem to fall into three categories:

1. Description of character or physical attribute/skill. Here are some examples of famous athlete's nicknames: *The Black Mamba* (basketball player Kobe Bryant), *The Big Hurt* (baseball player Frank Thomas), *The Big Unit* (baseball player Randy Johnson), *The Great One* (hockey player Wayne Gretzky), *Joe Cool* (football player Joe Montana), *Prime Time* (football player Deion Sanders).
2. Rhymes and name association. Examples of nicknames I've given guys over the years: *Big Deal* Neal; Nathan *Goose* Gossage (like the famous Yankee pitcher); *Captain* Curt (like "Kirk" of "Star Trek" fame); Tom *Perkins* (so named because he was always hanging out at the local Perkins restaurant. His actual last name is Stanziola).
3. Variations on first and/or last names.
   - First name extension examples: Marty - *Martin*; Ray - *Raymond*; Frank - *Franklin*; Shane - *Shaner*.
   - First name variation/association examples: Josh Buser - *Jiblets*, altered further to *Jibs*, and *Jibbles & Bits*; My son, Travis - *Chavez* (named after the Indian played by Lou Diamond Phillips in the movie *Young Guns*); Peter - *Petris*; Sam - *Samurai*.
   - Last name variation/association examples: Bob Mackley - *B-Mack*; Tom Harshberger - *Harshy*.
   - First, last or middle name only example: My best friend's first name is Cecil, which he hates. Only his close friends were allowed to call him Cecil; which made it cool.

~ Initials only examples (you know you've arrived if the world knows you by your initials!): Robert Griffin III - *RGIII;* Michael Jordan - *MJ;* Jim Wilt (a friend of mine) - *JW.*

~ Nicknames I've been called: *Wilson* (last name); *Wendell* (my dad's name); *Woodrow* (very presidential); *Waldo* (hated that one); *Wade-er* (not crazy about that one either); *PW* or *PDub* (short for Pastor Wayde).

Possible nicknames David and his Mighty Men might have given each other: Joshobeam - *Beamer;* Eleazar - *Zar, Z,* or *Z-Man;* Shammah - *Shammy* or *Sham-Wow;* Benaiah - *Benny, B-Dawg, Clubber* or *Samurai* (for disarming and killing a giant Egyptian with a club as his only weapon); Ithai - *Thai (like tie);* Zalmon - *Fish* or *Upstream* (c'mon, you get it!); Eliahba - *Eli;* Paarai – *Piranha;* Igal - *Iggy;* Uzziah - *Wizard* (of Uz) or *Wiz* (for short).

What nicknames have you been called (or are still called) by your buddies?

What were the nicknames of some of your friends growing up? (And what, if anything, did they mean?)

What are the nicknames of some of your current friends?

Your name or nickname is more than just the *identifying title* people call you; it's also an instant *reminder of your character* or *reputation*. The minute someone says your name, those who know you immediately pull up their personal history file of you.

The BIG IDEA for this chapter is *a man's name and his reputation are closely linked*. Let me give you some examples:

Positive-reputation: tough, hard-working, dedicated, honest, great father, loving husband, trusted friend, generous, good sense of humor.

Negative-reputation: cheater, liar, thief, selfish, lazy, slob, quitter, womanizer, drug addict, wife-beater, dead-beat dad, gambler, alcoholic, abusive.

 *In-Your-Face Challenge:*

What do people think of when they hear *your* name? (If you don't know, ask!)

In addition to the things (good and bad) that people think about us when they hear our names, are the negative names we think and believe about ourselves. Maybe they were said by a parent or stepparent, a teacher, or a coach. They may not be true, but they might as well be because they shape the way we *think* and *feel*— names like stupid, dumb, ignorant, ugly, worthless, clumsy...or maybe worse.

Here are a couple more questions for you:

Are you okay with the reputation connected to your name?

_____ YES _____ NO

If you answered no, then what are you going to do about it?

Maybe that last question is hard for you to answer. But you *can* do something to improve your reputation.

How to Have a Solid Gold Reputation

"A good name is worth more than silver or gold."[5]

In 2011, Ron Artest, who played in the National Basketball Association (NBA) for the Chicago Bulls, Indiana Pacers, Sacramento Kings, Houston Rockets, Los Angeles Lakers, and the New York Knicks, changed his name to Metta World Peace. According to Artest, "Changing my name was meant to inspire and bring youth together all around the world." That's an interesting explanation since Metta World Peace has often led the NBA in flagrant fouls, has been fined and suspended multiple times—including the longest suspension in NBA history (86 games) for an on-court brawl during the Pistons-Pacers game (November 19, 2004)—and has been arrested for domestic violence.

Changing your name won't necessarily improve your reputation. Metta World Peace is proof of that. So *what can you do* if you're not proud of the reputation associated with your name? I'm going to introduce you to two guys in the Bible who had bad reputations. The first is *Jacob*. Jacob's story is found in the Old Testament in Genesis, chapters 25-50. The second is *Saul*. His story is found in the New Testament beginning in Acts 7 through Acts 28. It would be great if you read their stories sometime, but since that would take a while, I'm going to summarize their lives down to one paragraph each.

Jacob's name meant "deceiver." Jacob and his twin brother, Esau, were bitter rivals who fought in their mother's womb before they were born![6] Esau was a big, hairy outdoorsman who loved to hunt. Jacob was a spoiled, sniveling Mama's boy who stayed in the house hanging on to his mother's apron strings. One day, with Mommy's help, Jacob deceived his blind, elderly father into believing he was Esau and stole his brother's birthright (the first-born son's inheritance). *Jacob's deceit tore his family apart.* He had to run for his life and never saw his mother again. Years later, preparing to face Esau the next day, Jacob got into an all-night wrestling match *with God.* Tired of the man he was, Jacob refused to let go of the Lord until he was different. He walked away from that encounter a changed man with a new name. *Jacob the Deceiver* became *Israel, "one who struggled with God and men and overcomes."* From that moment on, God changed Jacob's *character* along with his *name*.

Saul was a bounty hunter—for Christians; a vicious killer whose name and reputation was greatly feared in the early Church community. He believed Jesus Christ was a religious farce and a dangerous cult leader. Saul was so opposed to Christianity that he went from town to town rounding up Christ-followers and throwing them in jail, where many were tortured or killed. Saul stood by, enjoying the moment and holding the coats of the religious leaders while they stoned to death Stephen, the first martyr of the Church.[7] Saul was a bad man—until the day he met the resurrected Jesus face to face.[8] That encounter changed his life. *Saul the persecutor and murderer* became *Paul the missionary, God's "chosen instrument."*[9]

Paul became a fearless preacher of the Gospel, wrote half of the New Testament, started dozens of churches, and became one of the most influential Christian leaders of all time.

You *don't* have to change your name to change your reputation; but you *do* need God to change *you*. It won't be easy, but God has a proven record of making *great men* out of *bad guys!* Jacob and Saul's examples teach us three things we need to do if we want God to change the hard-to-change habits in our lives:

1. Surrender your pride. Men have big egos. We don't like to admit we're wrong or that we made a mistake. Until you humble yourself and get honest about your screw-ups and sins, no one can help you; not even God! That's why Alcoholics Anonymous meetings always begin with members introducing themselves like this, "Hi, my name is _____ and I'm an alcoholic." If you're too proud to admit your junk, then your junk will continue to define you—maybe for the rest of your life. Are you okay with that? Is your current reputation the way you want to be remembered? Sadly, it often takes a crisis to break us of our pride. And for some men, not even a crisis can do it. Don't be that guy.

2. Reach out for help. It's hard to reach out for help if you're hanging on to your pride. Clenched fists are hard to grasp. Open your hands and your heart and reach out to someone. Look especially for a guy who has faced the demons of his past and changed. There's help for you.

3. Refuse to make excuses or quit! Jacob and Saul's bad reputations were the result of years of bad habits. Changing their deeply ingrained patterns of behavior was one of the hardest things they ever faced. They could have made excuses: "This is just the way I am. I can't change." They could have easily fallen back into their old patterns. But when they had their God-encounters, they made a decision: I will not back off, make excuses or quit, *no matter what.* Read this next line very carefully: You don't *have* to stay the way you are; but you *will* stay that way until you determine to do *something different.*

Have you ever heard this line: *"More of the same never brings change"*? How about, *"The definition of insanity is doing the same thing the same way and expecting a different result"*? I know, even as I write this, more than one guy will get to this place and say, "But I've tried _____ and I've done _____ and it hasn't worked. I'm still the same."

What have you still *not* tried? Prayer? How about prayer and fasting?[10] Have you talked with a pastor or counselor? Have you checked yourself into a rehab center? Have you reached out to a couple of Christian guys, told them your story and asked them to hold you accountable?

If you've been fighting the same habits for years, do you think it's going to be easy to change? Nothing *worth doing* is easy! There will *always* be excuses and reasons why you "can't do it"; DO IT ANYWAY! You will fail and you will fall down; *get back up, refuse to quit, tell God you're counting on Him*, and KEEP GOING! Today is a great day to begin the change. Make the decision to let God change you *today,* or you will continue to be defined by the things you don't like *tomorrow* (and next week...next year...the year after that...and before you know it, the years add up to a lifetime).

The Bible says, *"It is better to be respected than to be rich. A good name is worth more than silver or gold."*[11] Mark Batterson, best-selling author[12] and pastor of National Community Church in Washington, DC, has a quote that goes like this, "I want to be famous in my own home." I like that. I want those who *know me best* to *respect me most;* and no one knows me more than my family. I hope I'm able to pass along a nice financial inheritance to my sons. But I'd rather leave them the example of a father who had good reputation than a jerk who left them lots of money. So with God's help, I'm working on a solid gold reputation. Believe me, I've got a long way to go! But hey, if God can turn a bunch of outlaws, a cheater (Jacob) and a beater (Saul) into heroes, why not me? *Why not you?*

Heaven's Hall of Fame

When you're standing in the hall of fame
And the world's gonna know your name
'Cause you burn with the brightest flame
And you'll be on the walls of the hall of fame.

There are more than 750 Halls, Walls, and Walks of Fame in the world. In addition to the more well-known Halls like the Pro Football HoF in Canton, Ohio, the National Baseball HoF in Cooperstown, New York, and the Rock and Roll HoF in Cleveland, Ohio, here are some you've probably never heard of; the Polka HoF, Mascot HoF, National Polish-American Sports HoF, Robot HoF, International Scuba Diving HoF, Consumer Electronics HoF, and more. It seems there's a Hall of Fame for nearly everything! There's even a *Dog Walk of Fame* in London, England!

All those Halls of Fame, and my name will most likely never be listed in any of them! *I'm okay with that.* But there's one list of names I want to be on more than anything. Having my name on this list would be the greatest honor, so it is my highest goal. I'm talking about a book in heaven called the *Book of Life* that lists the name of every person who has accepted Jesus Christ as their Lord and Savior. Here's a description of the *Book of Life:*

I saw the dead, great and small, standing before the throne, and books were opened. Another book was opened, which is the **book of life.** *The dead were judged according to what they had* *done as recorded in the books. The sea gave up the dead that were in it, and death and Hades gave up the dead that were in them, and each person was judged according to what they had done. Then death and Hades were thrown into the lake of fire. The lake of fire is the second death. Anyone whose name was not found written in the **book of life** was thrown into the lake of fire* (Revelation 20:12-15).

You can see after reading those verses, why it's so important to have your name listed in the *Book of Life*. It doesn't matter if you were inducted into several of this world's Halls of Fame; if your name's not in **God's book,** you're not getting into heaven. Not only are you banned from heaven for all eternity, you're thrown into what the Bible calls "the lake of fire." That's a hell of a place to spend eternity—literally. That's the bad news. The good news is that, thanks to Jesus, it's not hard to get your name listed in the *Book of Life.* Jesus did all the hard work when He suffered, bled, and died in your place on the cross.

All you have to do to get your name in the *Book of Life* is pray the prayer I told you about in Chapter 1 that you can find in Appendix A. When you make Jesus Christ *the* Leader of your life, God has heaven's official record keeper add your name to His Book.

And it gets even better! The Bible tells us that each of us will have a moment before the Lord in heaven when our names will be read aloud from the *Book of Life* before a great crowd of heaven's *Hall of Famers.*[13] All the great ones will be there: David and his Mighty Men, Jacob, Paul, and many more. And they'll all be cheering for *you* when God says, *"Well done, good and faithful servant!"*[14] That moment will be greater than any Hall of Fame induction ceremony on earth. Sometimes I dream about the moment when God will call my name. It motivates me.

You might be thinking, *It's too good to be true. A moment like that could never happen for me. You don't know the things I've done. I'm a royal screw-up. I don't deserve it.* I understand what you're feeling. I've made my share of mistakes too. But it's not *your reputation* that gets your name mentioned in heaven's Hall of Fame—it's *Jesus' reputation.* And His name and His reputation are spotless.[15] Thanks to Jesus, outlaws, cheaters, bounty hunters—and knuckle-heads like you and me—can one day find ourselves *standin' in the Hall of Fame...and God's gonna call our name.* It doesn't get any better than that.

If as a result of reading this chapter you made a commitment to let God change you from the inside until your name and your reputation honor Him, congratulations! You've won another victory in the Circle of Swords.

To Honor, To Courage, To Commitment...To God!

Sharpen your sword by memorizing this verse: *"It is better to be respected than to be rich. A good name is worth more than silver or gold"* (Proverbs 22:1 ERV).

CHAPTER

SECRET HIDEOUTS

David left Gath and escaped to the cave of Adullam...

1 SAMUEL 22:1 (NIV)

The Lord is my rock, my fortress and my deliverer; my God...in whom I take refuge...

PSALM 18:2 (NIV)

Big Idea: Where do you go to get away from it all with God and evaluate what's important in life?

Hideouts

My grandparent's hometown of Meade, Kansas, (population 1,651[1]) is the home of the Dalton Gang Hideout. The Dalton Gang,[2] so named because three of its members were Dalton brothers, was a group of Old West outlaws who specialized in bank and train robberies. Four of the Dalton Gang, including brothers Bob and Gratton Dalton, were killed in a gunfight when they attempted to rob two banks at the same time in broad daylight in Coffeyville, Kansas. Emmett Dalton, the only survivor, was shot twenty-three times. He did his prison time and eventually moved to California where he became an author, actor, and real estate agent. The Dalton Gang Hideout is a house formerly owned by the Dalton brothers' sister, Eva, and her husband, J.N. Whipple. Years after the couple left town, a secret underground tunnel was discovered running from the house to the barn. The Dalton Gang used the tunnel to come and go, undetected by the law. As a boy who loved stories about cowboys and Indians and the Wild West, I thought it was so cool that there was an outlaw hideout in the little town where my grandparents lived! We visited the Dalton Gang Hideout several times over the years when we went to see Grandpa and Grandma.

It's a guy thing to have hideouts, special, often secret locations where guys—good and bad—go to escape, make plans, and hang out. Here are a few famous hideouts: Batman's Batcave, Superman's Fortress of Solitude, The Little Rascal's He-Man Woman-Haters Clubhouse (No Girls Allowed!). Butch Cassidy and the Sundance Kid used three of the most famous Western outlaw hideouts: Hole-in-the-Wall in Wyoming, Brown's Park on the Colorado-Utah border, and Robber's Roost in Southeastern Utah. The top two pirate hideouts are Tortuga, Haiti (featured in the *Pirates of the Caribbean* movie) and Port Royal, Jamaica. All the bad guys in James Bond movies and in comic books have secret hideouts.

Can you think of other famous hideouts?

Which famous hideout would you most like to visit?

Why?

When I was a boy, my buddies and I had our own secret hideouts. All of them were located on several acres of government-owned property called the Great Plains Field Station,[3] two blocks up the street from my house in Woodward, Oklahoma. One of our hideouts was called the Vine Tree. It was a tree with a large canopy that was completely overgrown with wild grape vines. The vines were so thick we could climb them and sit on top of the tree. It was *awesome*. I've climbed lots of trees, but that's the only tree I've ever sat on *top* of! Underneath the Vine Tree was our Underground Escape hideout.[4] We dug a hole in the ground big enough to hold three or four boys, covered it with plywood and added a layer of dirt, leaves, and sticks to hide it. A big tumbleweed hid the entrance hole.[5] There were candles in little recesses in the walls and comic books to read. It was dark and quiet and smelled like dirt. I loved hanging out in our secret underground hideout.

We had one more hideout we called The Fort. It was a recessed area surrounded by trees. We made dried mud balls for throwing at "enemies" who might attack us, and set several booby-traps for unfortunate guys who tried to raid the place when we weren't around to defend it. Many hours of my childhood were spent in and around these hideouts; playing games, setting old steel traps baited with Chex Mix[6] (we caught several squirrels and one *mean* possum!), shooting BB guns and slingshots—boy stuff. Those hideouts were some of my favorite places. Memories of them still bring a smile to my face (and a sigh of relief that I didn't get caught and in trouble for some of the stupid things we did!).

Did you have a secret hideout of some kind when you were a boy?

_____ YES   _____ NO

What was it like (was it a tree house, underground, a clubhouse, etc.)?

Who besides you knew about the hideout (which of your friends were in on the hideout)?

What did you do (what kind of imaginary games, activities, etc.) when you were hanging out in your secret hideout?

Man Caves

The idea of boyhood *hideouts* has evolved into the modern trend of *man caves*. A man cave, sometimes called a manland, mantuary, or man space, is a male sanctuary. It is not an actual cave, but rather a room inside the house, the basement, garage, attic, or office; or outside the house such as a wood shed, tool room, or hunting cabin where guys can do as they please. A man cave has multiple purposes: a place to be alone, away from women and female house rules; work on hobbies, and hang out with friends to watch sports or play video games.

Man caves are often equipped with accessories like refrigerators, vending machines, putting greens, giant TVs complete with surround sound system, musical instruments including gear such as microphone stands and amplifiers, pool tables, and even boxing rings! A man cave may also be fitted with a bar and sports memorabilia such as trophies, pictures, fatheads,[7] and furniture in honor of your favorite team(s). (There are some awesome pictures of man caves out there on the Internet!) Man caves have become so popular that there's a home renovation reality television show devoted to man caves on the DIY Network hosted by former NFL defensive tackle and Super Bowl winner Tony Siragusa and licensed contractor, Jason Cameron.

According to psychiatrist and author Scott Haltzman, "It is important for a man to have a place to call his own in which to retreat." Some psychologists claim a man cave can provide refuge from stressful surroundings and be beneficial to marriage. (I'm sure lots of guys will be using *that* line as a selling point to their wife for building a man cave!) It's a way for married men to recreate some of the space and freedom of their bachelor days; similar to a bachelor pad, frat house, or college dorm room where guys could come and go "as if they owned the place." In his book *Where Men Hide*, author James Twitchell says man caves are possibly, "a modern-day replacement for declining attendance at male-only clubs such as Masonic Lodges," noting that some anthropologists have speculated that these spots are a place for men to bond before hunting or war, and where they can "smoke or fart" and tell the "same jokes over and over again."

Do you have some type of man cave getaway?

_____ YES   _____ NO

What's your favorite thing about your man cave?

Adullam: David's Man Cave

David and His Mighty Men had a *real* man cave; a secret hideout called the cave of Adullam.

Here's a description of David's man cave:

> *The cave which frequently served as the secret headquarters for David and his four-to-six-hundred men was located in the Judean wilderness in the general area where Scripture says David hid from King Saul. The cavern is on a long, narrow ledge high above the bottom of a ravine. Nearby is a spring of clear, cool running water. The only access to the cave is through a circular opening some seven feet high. One large broken rock, weighing many tons, almost bars the entrance. Inside, massive fragments of rock lay about on the cavern floor. There is a narrow, low passage leading to a small cave, from which a winding passage leads to a large room of about five thousand square feet. Narrow passages branch out and lead to other large rooms, some of which are on lower levels. There is ample room within for a thousand men.*[8]

Does that sound like a cool hideout or what?! Sure, if you're used to living in the king's palace like David had been, sleeping in a cave is several steps down. But a cave was the perfect headquarters for an outlaw army. Can't you just imagine all those battle-hardened warriors sitting around, roasting meat over the fire, laughing and telling stories late into the night as the flames flickered shadows on the cave walls? *I can almost smell the smoke.* David and his men bonded with one another during those dark nights in their man cave. But Adullam wasn't just David's military headquarters and the secret hideout where he and his men went to escape from King Saul; it was also a place where David connected with God.

Hiding Out with God

The cave of Adullam was a place of safety for David. When you're running for your life, I'm sure it's a good feeling to have a safe place where you can go and relax—at least for a little while. Strangely enough, during those hard years when he was hiding in caves, David was really close to God. Someone said, "Had David prayed as much in his *palace* (when he became king) as he did in his *cave* (when he was running for his life), he might never have fallen into the act that brought such misery upon his latter days" (referring to his sin of adultery with Bathsheba).

When you're going through a hard time, you have a choice; you can either *push away* from God, or *move toward* Him. David chose to move toward God. In fact, David came to realize that the cave of Adullam wasn't his most secure hiding place—*God was*. God was his refuge in times of trouble. David learned that if he wasn't with God, no cave, no castle, no fortress, no hideout, *no place on earth* was safe. And so, sitting somewhere in the darkness of his secret hideout, David wrote Psalm 57 and 142. Here's how David describes God:

> *Have mercy on me, my God...for* **in you I take refuge. I will take refuge in the shadow of your wings** *until the disaster has passed* (Psalm 57:1).

> *When I am overwhelmed, you alone know the way I should turn. Wherever I go, my enemies have set traps for me. I look for someone to come and help me, but no one gives me a passing thought! No one will help me; no one cares a bit what happens to me. Then I pray to you, O Lord. I say, "**You are my place of refuge.** You are all I really want in life"* (Psalm 142:3-5 NLT).

And living in a cave...running for his life...confused by circumstances he didn't understand...unsure what the next day had in store for him...*David could rest*, knowing he was safe because *God had his back*. God was his Hiding Place. Better than any secret hideout on earth, *God is a safe place in a world filled with trouble.*

We've talked about boyhood hideouts and man cave getaways. But here's a big question for you: *When and where do you go to get alone with God?* Life gets confusing and hard; overwhelming at times. We find ourselves on the run from the fear of failure, from the reality of a bad marriage, from trying to keep up with the world's standards of success. In the hectic pace of life, it's easy to lose track of who we are and let our priorities get all messed up. I don't care how sweet your man cave is, you can't escape from the realities of life for long.

But if God is your Hiding Place, He'll have your back, He'll lead you out of dark places, and He'll keep you from losing sight of the things that matter. But you've got to get with Him.

 ***In-Your-Face Challenge:***

When was the last time you spent some quality time with God?

Plan a Spiritual Getaway with God

As a deer thirsts for streams of water, so I thirst for you, God. I thirst for the living God. **When can I go to meet with him?** (Psalm 42:1-2 NCV)

I challenge you to set aside some time; a day or a weekend, to hide out and hang out with God. You may have never done anything like this, so you don't have a clue where to begin. Don't sweat it. In Appendix B you'll find ideas and questions to help you plan a Spiritual Getaway with God based on Four Rs:

Rest...from your hectic schedule/routine
Reconnect...with God
Reevaluate...your priorities
Recommit...to the things that matter most

Life is going to keep coming at you. Days will become weeks, and weeks will become years. If you don't make the time to dream and plan and evaluate your priorities, no one else is going to do it for you. Mark Batterson, a big fan of spiritual getaways, has come up with a phrase to describe the positive results of getting away with God:

Change of Pace + Change of Place = Change of Perspective

If you will commit to pull away from all the distractions and the hectic pace of your life to hide out and hang out with God, you will come back from the experience a changed man—energized, focused, confident, a better husband, father, friend. Best and most important, you'll come back closer to God. So don't put it off. Don't make excuses. JUST DO IT.

I commit to meet with God:

Date(s): _____ A day is great; a weekend (Friday night, Saturday, return Sunday) is better! Don't rush it.

Place: _____ Make sure it's a place where you won't be interrupted.

If, as a result of reading this chapter, you made a commitment to get away and meet with God, congratulations! You've won another victory in the Circle of Swords.

To Honor, To Courage, To Commitment...To God!

Sharpen your sword by memorizing this verse: *"The Lord is my rock, my fortress and my deliverer; my God...in whom I take refuge"* (Psalm 18:2a).

CHAPTER

You've Got Skillz!

...several brave warriors joined him [David] to help fight his battles. ...They were experts at using a bow and arrows, and they could shoot an arrow or sling a stone with either hand.

1 Chronicles 12:1-2 (CEV)

Christ has given each of us special abilities...

Ephesians 4:7 (TLB)

Big Idea: Every man has God-given abilities that can make a difference in the world.

Mad Skillz

Mad Skillz is defined as an extreme amount of skill in a specific area (Source: Urban Dictionary).

In the movie *Taken*, retired but still lethal CIA agent Bryan Mills (played by actor Liam Neeson) has a brief phone conversation with one of the ruthless gang members who have just abducted his teenage daughter. That scene is my favorite part of the movie. Here's what he says:

> I don't know who you are. I don't know what you want. If you are looking for ransom, I can tell you I don't have money. But what I do have are a very particular set of skills; skills I have acquired over a very long career. Skills that make me a nightmare for people like you. If you let my daughter go now, that'll be the end of it. I will not look for you, I will not pursue you. But if you don't, I will look for you, I will find you, and I will kill you.

After a long pause, the kidnapper simply says, "Good luck" in a heavy foreign accent and hangs up. From that moment, it's game on. Relying on his "very particular set of skills," Bryan Mills tracks down the gang, who are kidnapping and forcing young girls into the sex-slave industry, launching a one-man war to bring them to justice. It's an intense movie. True to his word, Mills gets his daughter back and, through voice recognition (he recorded their brief conversation), takes out the man he threatened on the phone. Bryan Mills has *mad skillz*.

So did David's Mighty Men. Wolverine, the mutant superhero and member of the X-Men, is famous for saying, "I'm the best at what I do."[1] That describes David's elite group of super soldiers. They were the best of the best; skilled warriors who had developed their abilities to the highest level—the Green Beret/Navy SEAL/Special Ops Forces of David's army.[2] Check out some of the descriptions of these guys:

Jashobeam, Eleazar, and Shammah (David's top three Mighty Men) each single-handedly defeated hundreds of enemy soldiers in hand-to-hand combat. *Jashobeam* killed eight hundred men in one battle![3]

The Big Three also broke through enemy lines once just to get David a drink of water from his favorite well in Bethlehem.[4]

Abishai, the commander or general of David's armies, once "raised his spear against three hundred men, who he killed."[5]

Benaiah took out two of Moab's best soldiers, snatched the spear from a giant Egyptian (seven and a half feet tall!), killed him with his own weapon, and "went down into a pit on a snowy day and killed a lion."[6] He was such a bad dog that David made him his personal bodyguard.

Here's a description of the skilled soldiers David recruited and trained:

> *They were experts at using a bow and arrows, and they could shoot an arrow or sling a stone with either hand. The weakest among them could take on a hundred regular troops, and the strongest could take on a thousand!*[7]

These guys' skill level was off the charts. They were *scary good.* I admire guys who are the best at what they do. But I'll be honest, some guys are so good, smart, and talented that it can make me feel...well, pretty *average.* For example, have you ever looked at some complicated invention like a computer or a space shuttle—or even something like a light bulb, and thought, *How was someone smart enough to figure out how to make that?!* I have trouble understanding and using all the features on my iPhone, but somebody was so smart he figured out how to assemble little pieces of metal and plastic and create a device that can sort, receive, send, and hold millions of pieces of information that fits in the palm of my hand. It blows my mind. If, like me, you've ever felt like, *I don't have mad skillz; I'm not really that good at anything,* keep reading, because the Bible says...

You've Got Skillz

My 17-year-old son, Travis, has a T-shirt that says: *My skills pay the bills.* I love that shirt—and I really love my son, but so far, his skills haven't paid *any* of the bills. In fact, *my* skills pay the bills (for things like milk and clothes!). But I know Travis has God-given skills, and I can't wait to see them develop in the coming years. My oldest son, Trevor, has become really good at home improvement: wiring, plumbing, roofing, siding, framing, drywall, etc. When he graduated from high school he didn't know how to do any of that stuff. But Trevor pursued his interest, learned by apprenticing under a couple of great carpenters, and now he's making a living with the skills he's developed.

The Bible says, *"Christ has given each of us special abilities."*[8] I want you to stop right here and think about the things you're good at. It might be a skill(s) you've learned that helps you earn a living, or it might be something you're good at that has nothing to do with your job. Maybe you play a mean guitar, make furniture, design computer graphics, take great pictures, or you're really good at fixing cars. I even want you to include things like being really good at hunting, fishing, and other recreational sports. Are you ready?

What are your skillz, the things you're naturally good at?

What do you love to do (your interests)?

Not only does the Bible say we've all got skillz, it also says God gave us these skills, abilities, and interests so that we can make a positive difference for Him in the world. Here's an example of what I'm talking about, *"It is God himself who has made us what we are and given us new lives from Christ Jesus; and long ages ago he planned that we should spend these lives helping others."*[9] In his best-selling book *What On Earth Am I Here For?,* author and pastor Rick Warren writes:

> You were put on earth to make a contribution. You weren't just created to consume resources—to eat, breath and take up space. God designed you to make a difference with your life. While many best-selling books offer advice on how to *'get'* the most out of life, that's not the reason God made you. You were created to *add* life on earth, not just take from it. God wants you to give something back."[10]

In simplest terms, God has given you *a very particular set of skills* and one lifetime to discover, develop, and use those skills to make a difference in this broken, hurting world. That's one of the main reasons you're alive. It would be a tragedy to live your whole life and never know what they were—or to know what they were, but *only use them for selfish reasons.* I could give you all kinds of examples of men whose amazing skills made them rich and famous, yet they died having never, or only partially, fulfilled their God-given potential. Don't let that happen to you. God has given you skills, a special assignment, and with His help *the mission is possible.*

But you will face opposition.

Skill Killers

Jesus told us that we have an enemy. In fact, He even described our enemy's strategy: *"The thief's* [Satan's] *purpose is to steal and kill and destroy. My purpose is to give...a rich and satisfying life."*[11] Every day, in every way, Satan wants to rip you off and take you down. If you knew how much Satan hates you, it would make you so angry you'd wake up every day fighting mad. Whenever you see human beings at their worst, doing the most horrific things imaginable—raping and abusing little children, selling teenage girls as sex slaves, brutally torturing and murdering people—things that make your skin crawl and your stomach turn and cause you to think, *How could anyone do something like that?* That's the work of Satan. He uses people as his pawns to accomplish his purpose: to steal, kill, and destroy.

Have I got your attention? *Satan is the guy* who wants to *steal your potential,* keep you from accomplishing God's purpose for your life, turn you against God, and if you let him—*drag you to hell with him.* Sound harsh? *You have no idea.* And yet, Satan is so slick and subtle that many times when he's ripping us off and wrecking our lives, we don't even recognize it's him. I get sick of seeing it happen. I'm ticked off right now just thinking of the lives he has destroyed; the talent and potential he has thrown away. So I'm fighting while I'm writing—fighting for *you.* I stopped writing right here to pray that God would grab your heart and inspire you to step up and **be the man God created you to be.**

You've got skillz (Ephesians 4:7) and you were made for a mission (Ephesians 2:10), but if you're going to become the skilled warrior God created you to be, you need to be aware of and ready to fight Satan's attempts to steal and destroy your God-given potential. The Bible also says, *we are familiar with Satan's evil schemes so that he will not outsmart us.*[12] Here are some of Satan's most common skill killers: ignorance, comparisons, distractions, selfishness, and weakness.

Ignorance (lack of understanding) – If you didn't *know God* and you had never heard or read the verses from the Bible that you just read, you could have gone your whole life without knowing

God made you for a mission and gave you a very specific set of skills to accomplish that mission. That's the first big secret Satan wants to keep from you. What you *don't know* won't *hurt him* and *his evil plans* for the world. But now that you know *you've got skills*, the next step is to discover and develop them. David's Mighty Men were already skilled warriors, but through continuous training and development, they became *"experts at using a bow and arrows, and they could shoot an arrow or sling a stone with either hand."*

One of the best tools I've ever seen for helping someone discover and develop their God-given potential is the SHAPE assessment. This tool is great because it not only helps you discover your skills (the A in SHAPE or your Abilities), it also helps you discover your:

- **S**piritual Gifts (God-empowered abilities given to believers)
- **H**eart (what you love to do and care about most)
- **A**bilities (the skillz or natural talents you were born with)
- **P**ersonality (your uniqueness; there's *no one like you* and God wants to use you uniquely)
- **E**xperiences (God uses the things we've been through, good and *bad,* to help others)

For more information about the SHAPE assessment, go to www.saddlebackresources.com.

Comparisons – Comparing leads to one of two negative reactions: *pride* or *envy.* You can always find someone you think you're better than, and it will make you *prideful.* On the other hand, you will always find people you think are better than you, and you will become *envious* and discouraged. The Bible says, *"When they measure themselves by themselves and compare themselves to themselves, they show how foolish they are."*[13] The important question to ask yourself is, "Am I doing what God created me to do and making the most of what I've been given?"

Distractions – Distractions aren't necessarily evil things. They can be good or bad. For example, hunting, fishing, watching sports, spending time with your girlfriend aren't bad things (unless you've got a girlfriend *and you're married*...in that case, we need to talk!). But if things like that distract you from doing what God put you on the planet to do, then you have let too many good things keep you from accomplishing the most important things. There's a verse in the Bible that describes how short life is: *"What is your life? You are a mist that appears for a little while and then vanishes."*[14] You've only got one lifetime; ***don't waste it*** on distractions.

Selfishness – We're naturally selfish. We think of ourselves—our needs, our comfort, and our desires—first and most often. That's one of the effects sin has on us. Selfishness is a skill killer that makes us think our abilities and blessings are for our benefit. How...selfish. I agree with Rick Warren: "You weren't just created to consume resources...God wants you to give something back." You've been blessed to be a blessing. It feels great when God uses you to help someone else. The thief (Satan) doesn't want you to experience that feeling. So he'll keep you focused on you. You don't know what you're missing! It's time to find out.

Weakness (self-doubt) – "I'm not good at anything. I'm not smart. I'm not talented. I can't." STOP IT! The Bible is full of guys who thought they weren't good enough for God to use.[15] DON'T MISS THIS: *God will accomplish more good in the world through a seemingly untalented man whose heart is fully surrendered to Him than He can ever accomplish through an incredibly talented man who is full of himself.* The apostle Paul learned that God is so great He can even turn our weaknesses into strengths.[16]

Use Me

In the Old Testament, a man named Isaiah saw the Lord in a vision.[17] It messed him up pretty bad. God's holiness made Isaiah feel very un-holy and un-worthy. But God took away Isaiah's sin, and then He asked him a question (two actually): *"Whom should I send as a messenger to the people? And who will go for us?"* Isaiah responded, *"Here I am. Send me!"* I want you to put yourself in Isaiah's shoes. Imagine God saying to you, *"I'm looking for a volunteer for an assignment. Do you know someone?"* Before you answer, I want to make something clear: God *already knew* Isaiah was the man for the job—just like He already knows you've got what it takes to do what He's asking you. He's already chosen you. But now, *the God of the universe* is waiting for your response. So, *what's your answer?*

 ***In-Your-Face Challenge:***

Will you let God use your skills and passions to make a difference in this broken, hurting world? If your answer is yes, then I challenge you to push aside every fear and excuse and say this prayer:

God, USE ME! Everything *I have,* everything *I am*...it all belongs to You. So I give it back to You. Remove every obstacle. Remove every excuse. Free me from comparisons, distractions, selfishness, and insecurity. Open the doors, point the way, show me who You want me to serve, and USE ME. Thank You, Lord. Amen.

I once heard someone say, *"The most dangerous prayer you can pray is, 'Lord, use me!'"* You have just given God, who has *limitless power,* full access to your life! You have no idea how God might use you *today!* Just stay available. Pray throughout the day, *"God, keep my heart and my eyes open to needs around me."* I encourage you to take the SHAPE assessment, and after you do, talk to your pastor or someone in leadership at your church. Let them know how you scored and that you're available and want God to use you. And when God uses you, be sure to thank Him and give Him the credit.

Every time a man says, *"God, use my life for Your glory,"* the Circle of Swords grows stronger. Like David's Mighty Men, you are committed to becoming a skilled warrior for the Lord.

To Honor, To Courage, To Commitment...To God!

Sharpen your sword by memorizing this verse: *"Be sure to use the abilities God has given you...Put these abilities to work..."* (1 Timothy 4:14-15 Living Bible).

CHAPTER 5

BRAVEHEART

These were the men who came to David...while he was banished from the presence of Saul... They were brave warriors, ready for battle...their faces were the faces of lions...

1 Chronicles 12:1,8 (NIV)

With him [God] on my side I'm fearless, afraid of no one and nothing.

David in Psalm 27:1b (MSG)

I looked for a man from among them who would... stand in the gap before me on behalf of the land, so that I would not have to destroy it, but I found no one.

Ezekiel 22:30 (NET)

Big Idea: Deep in the heart of every man is the desire to do something heroic.

What Courage Looks Like

"Courage is being scared to death, but saddling up anyway."
–John Wayne

I hope heaven has time machines. After studying and writing about David's Mighty Men, I'd like to see them in action. Not the cleaned-up-for-heaven version; I want to see them *just before a battle.* Dirty, sweaty, banging their swords on their shields. Adrenaline pumping. Fingers twitching. Muscles flexing. The Bible says, *"Their faces were the faces of lions...."* I want to see the fire in their eyes and hear them roar; yelling and getting in each other's faces like football players before they take the field for a big game. I want to feel their intensity and be intimidated by their courage.

Before the final battle in the movie *King Arthur,*[1] the castle gate opens and Arthur, in full battle-armor, rides out through the smoke on a big white horse to meet Cerdic, the Saxon chief. It's an awesome scene. Both men are intimidating in their own way. Neither shows any fear. Here's the exchange that takes place between the two:

Cerdic (standing on the ground): "You come to beg a truce. You should be on your knees."

Arthur (on horseback, pointing his sword at Cerdic): "I came to see your face so that I alone may find you on the battlefield. And it will be good of you to mark my face, Saxon. For the next time you see it, it will be the last thing you see on this earth."

Cerdic (as Arthur rides off and Cerdic turns to walk back toward his troops): "Ahhh, finally. A man worth killing."

The battle that follows is brutal; hand-to-hand combat with swords, spears, and shields. That's how David and his Mighty Men fought. Man on man. Swords clanging, men yelling and swearing, blood splattering, people dying all around. I have often watched reenactments of battles like that and thought to myself, *I'm glad I've never had to fight in a war.* And I wonder how I would have performed and what emotions a soldier must feel in those last moments before he puts his life on the line.

David and his Mighty Men fought like that again and again. *That's what courage looks like*; a soldier laying his life on the line. But that's not the only face of courage. Courage comes in many forms. Courage looks like a...

- New York City firefighter running into the World Trade Center on 9/11/2001
- student standing up for another student against the schoolyard bully
- president taking an unpopular stand against slavery (Abraham Lincoln)
- preacher fighting for racial equality (Martin Luther King Jr.)
- fighter who's been knocked to the canvas getting up for another round
- husband who refuses to give up on his marriage when things get tough
- man who was laid off after 25 years who finds another job
- worker who blows the whistle on corporate corruption
- stranger who rescues someone from a burning vehicle
- missionary who leaves everything comfortable to share the Gospel in a foreign land
- Christian who is tortured, imprisoned, or killed for his or her faith in Christ
- child battling cancer
- parent of a child battling cancer

- teenager who stands up against peer pressure
- shepherd boy with a slingshot taking on a giant

Courage has many faces. What does courage look like to you? (Write your answers here.)

Where Courage Comes From

We recognize courage when we see it. It instantly inspires us. But where does courage come from? Courage is created by a CAUSE: *the determination to defend what is right* or *the willingness to protect something—or someone—valuable.* David's Mighty Men fought for God, and for David, the man they knew was God's anointed leader. When David became king, they fought for their country, for honor, for their families, and for each other. They were motivated by the *causes* they believed in.

- A stranger will run into a burning building for a stranger, beCAUSE a human being is valuable.
- A sick person will battle disease, beCAUSE life is worth living.
- A president and a preacher will fight against racism, risking their lives, beCAUSE no one should be treated less than another because their skin is a different color.
- A student will stand up to a bully beCAUSE he doesn't like to see someone taken advantage of.
- A man who is laid off will find another job, beCAUSE he has a family to take care of.
- An employee will risk losing his job to expose corporate corruption, beCAUSE he values principles over his paycheck.
- A husband will fight for his marriage, beCAUSE he made a commitment "til death do us part."

- A missionary will go to a foreign land, beCAUSE everyone deserves to hear that God sent His Son to save us from our sins.
- A soldier will make the ultimate sacrifice, beCAUSE freedom is worth fighting and dying for.

In the war film *Braveheart,*[2] Mel Gibson portrays William Wallace, a 13th-century Scottish warrior who led the Scots in the First War of Scottish Independence against King Edward I of England. Here is the dialogue from one of the most memorable scenes in the movie when William Wallace inspires his fellow Scotsmen to fight for their freedom:

William Wallace: "I am William Wallace! And I see a whole army of my countrymen, here in defiance of tyranny. You've come to fight as free men...and free men you are. *What will you do with that freedom?* Will you fight?"

Veteran: "Fight? Against that?" [The superior English army] "No! We will run. And we will live."

William Wallace: "Aye, fight and you may die. Run, and you'll live...at least a while. And dying in your beds, many years from now, would you be willin' to trade ALL the days, from this day to that, for one chance, *just one chance,* to come back here and tell our enemies that they may take our lives, *but they'll never take...OUR FREEDOM!"*

[Scottish army cheers.]

William Wallace: "Alba gu bràth!" ["Scotland forever!"]

Wallace is eventually tried for high treason and condemned to public torture and beheading. Even while being hanged, drawn, and quartered, Wallace refuses to beg for mercy and submit to the English king. As the watching crowd cries for mercy, deeply moved by the Scotsman's valor, the magistrate offers him one final chance, asking him only to utter the word "Mercy" and be granted a quick death. But instead of mercy, Wallace shouts *"FREEDOM!"* and the judge orders his death. The *cause* of freedom fueled William Wallace's courage and led his fellow Scotsmen to a stunning defeat of the English.

Courage is created by a cause. *"Faced with what is right, to leave it undone shows a lack of courage."* –Confucius

Something Worth Fighting For

If courage is created by a cause, then the question for you if you truly want to be a Mighty Man of God, is this: Is there not a cause in this world worth fighting for?

The BIG IDEA for this chapter is *deep in the heart of every man is the desire to do something heroic.* I believe that. God built into men the spirit of a warrior; a defender. But without a cause to fight for, there's no adventure—no sense of purpose. Our lives become dull and meaningless. We get up day after day and just go through the motions. Men who were meant to wield swords and defend honor are reduced to pencil pushers; nameless, faceless employees working for the weekend. Deep inside we long for more. We long for *a challenge* that motivates us, *an adventure* that sends adrenaline rushing through our veins, *a cause* that scares us half to death but makes us feel alive.

When they were living on the run, David and his Mighty Men woke up every day facing the reality that *this day could be our last.* You might think, *That's no way to live!* And I say, *"It's the only way to live! The day you wake up without a sword in your hand and a cause worth fighting for is the day you begin to die while you're still living."* I'll guarantee you, if you could hang out with David's Mighty Men years later when they were older and God had given them a time of hard-earned peace from war, they didn't sit around talking about the boring days when they had nothing to do but guard the palace! No, they talked about the days when they lived in caves, ran for their lives, took on giants, and defeated their enemies. Those were the times when they were most alive! Every day was an adventure.

And so I ask you again, *Is there not a cause in this world worth fighting for?* If you want to do something brave, you must *find it* and *take it on.* Courage never shows up until there's *an obstacle* to overcome, *a villain* to be vanquished, *a wrong* to be made right, *an innocent victim* to protect. "Where" you ask, "do I find such a cause? Where do I find something worth fighting for?" In the previous chapter, I told you Jesus said we have an enemy named Satan whose purpose is *"to steal, kill and destroy."*[3] If you're looking for a cause that requires courage, then with God's help and in Jesus' name, STOP HIM! You want a cause worth fighting for? Then step up and fight any one of these:

Hunger. Lack of clean drinking water. Disease. These three causes are killing millions of people around the world every day. They need a hero to bring them food, medicine...a drink of water. You want a holy cause? Fight *prostitution* and *sex-slave trafficking.* Men who are cowards are running those "businesses"; the world needs men of courage to step up and shut them down.

There are worthy causes all around you! Satan is on the move spreading *addiction, alcoholism, poverty, abuse, abortion, pornography, homelessness, racism, slavery, prejudice, corruption, the break-up of the home, fatherless children, religious hypocrisy...the list goes on and on.* The enemy is on a rampage and men have laid down their swords for remote controls and cell phones. We're too busy, we're too soft, and we've stopped being brave.

I pray to God that I will do something bold and courageous in the name of the Lord before I die! Something that makes my *knees knock* and my *heart pound* and my *stomach sick* because it's so hard and so crazy that I can't do it on my own—but so right and so worth doing that God steps in and wins the battle. I want to stare down the enemy for a holy cause. I want to *live*, not just *exist*. I don't need to be a hero, but I *am* asking God to give me a brave heart.

> *"The brave may not live forever, but the cautious do not live at all."* –Meg Cabot

The Making of a Braveheart

> *"I learned that courage was not the absence of fear, but the triumph over it."* –Nelson Mandela

> *"Give me one hundred preachers who fear nothing but sin and desire nothing but God, and I care not a straw whether they be clergymen or laymen, such alone will shake the gates of hell and set up the kingdom of heaven upon earth."* –John Wesley

You may be thinking, *But I'm no hero.* It might help you to know that pretty much every guy who has ever done something courageous didn't think of themselves as a hero at the time when they did something brave. They simply responded to a need or a cry for help.

There's a verse in the Bible that goes so well with this chapter. God's people, the Israelites, had once again turned their backs on Him. Their sin was causing all kinds of pain and problems in society; things like murder, bribery, corruption, extortion, robbery, and poverty.[4] In other words, there were plenty of causes creating opportunities for someone with godly courage to step up. It got so bad that God was ready to bring divine judgment on His people—always His last resort, because God is a God of grace and mercy. But before He sent His judgment down, God said something interesting, *"I looked for a man among them* [my people] *who would...stand before me in the gap on behalf of the land so I would not have to destroy it, but I found no one."*[5]

Let that sink in. God said: If I could have found just *one man* who was willing take a stand against sin, I would have used him to save the nation. Notice God does not say, "I was looking for a *brave* man..." God doesn't need you to be a *hero;* He just needs you to *be a man!* If God can just find a *willing* man, He will put His braveheart into that man and *make* him a hero. How do I know this? Because when He couldn't find a man courageous enough to save the world from sin, God *became* that man—sacrificing His own *brave*heart on the cross. He's ready to help anyone who will take a stand against Satan. David wrote, *"With God on my side I'm fearless, afraid of no one and nothing."*[6] It's time to get in your face again.

 ***In-Your-Face Challenge:***

What brave thing would you do for God in the world if you knew you couldn't fail? (Examples: end slavery or world hunger, cure AIDS, help fatherless kids, etc.)

Maybe you picked something so big that it seems impossible. Sometimes it helps to break big dreams down to reasonable goals. What is one positive thing you can do to make a difference? (Example: You may not be able to cure AIDS, but you could help one person who has AIDS.)

Sometimes the bravest thing needed is to confront our own issues. Are there any "giants" (addictions, habits, sins) in your life that you need to fight?

I'm proud to know some modern-day bravehearts. Like Dave Wellman. Dave retired early from the police force, raised support, sold his home and moved his family to Nicaragua to oversee an orphanage with Metanoia Missions International. His buddies on the force thought he was crazy, but Dave is a braveheart.

In 2003, Mickey Minnich lost his wife, Vickie, the love of his life, to cancer. Mickey courageously turned his tragedy into triumph by creating Vickie's Angel Foundation, Inc., a 501(c)(3) non-profit organization with the mission of helping families having difficulties paying the bills as their loved one battles cancer.

Another braveheart is Steve Engle. Steve and his wife, Lori, are foster parents who have adopted several children over the years. As if adoption isn't already courageous enough, Steve and Lori have made it a point to adopt several special needs children—some with severe physical handicaps. The love, patience, and sacrifice on display in their home is something to see! God only knows where the children the Engle's have adopted would be if this courageous man and woman had not entered their lives. Steve doesn't think of himself as a hero, but I do.

I also know many men who travel around the world using their vacation time and paying for their own transportation and lodging to build (and following natural disasters, rebuild) homes, schools, churches, medical centers, etc. These guys are just average Joe's back here in the states, but they're heroes in places like Haiti and Tanzania and Burkina Faso, Africa where they showed up and changed the lives (in some cases, *saved* the lives) of people they may never see again until heaven. Such men are bravehearts. And God wants to add *you* to the list!

Here's a great quote from Jon Acuff, *"When I become brave, I'll let you know. Until then, I'm just going to do a lot of awesome things scared out of my mind."* There's a real enemy waging war just outside your front door. The innocent suffer, lost people are dying, a broken world is waiting...and God is searching *for a man*. Will you step forward? Will you put your sword in the circle? Take a bold step in God's direction and He will put His braveheart in you. And together, you and God will do something courageous in the world.

> *"Don't be afraid of your fears. They're not there to scare you. They're there to let you know that something is worth it."*
> –C JoyBell C

> *"Since it's so likely that children will meet cruel enemies, let them at least have heard of brave knights and heroic courage."*
> –C.S. Lewis

To Honor, To Courage, To Commitment...To God!

Sharpen your sword by memorizing this verse: *"Be strong and courageous. Do not be terrified; do not be discouraged, for the Lord your God will be with you wherever you go"* (Joshua 1:9).

CHAPTER

TRUE FRIENDS

Once a group of men...went out to the fort where David was. David went out to meet them and said, "If you are coming as friends to help me, you are welcome here. Join us! But if you intend to betray me to my enemies, even though I have not tried to hurt you, the God of our ancestors will know it and punish you." God's spirit took control of one of them, Amasai, who later became the commander of "The Thirty," and he called out, "David son of Jesse, we are yours! Success to you and those who help you! God is on your side." David welcomed them and made them officers in his army.

1 Chronicles 12:16-18 (Good News Translation)

The greatest love a person can show is to die for his friends.

John 15:13 (NCV)

Big Idea: What are the characteristics of a true friend and do you have them?

The Stuff Friends Are Made Of

You can count on me like 1 2 3
I'll be there
And I know when I need it
I can count on you like 4 3 2
And you'll be there
Cause that's what friends are supposed to do, oh yeah.
–"Count on Me" by Bruno Mars

"A good friend is hard to find, hard to lose, and impossible to forget..." –Unknown

"Associate yourself with people of good quality, for it is better to be alone than in bad company." –Unknown

You only get a handful of really good friends in a lifetime. You can't buy them (if you do, they're not true friends). It takes a lot of time and a variety of real-life experiences to test the quality of them. Eventually, if you live *long* enough—and *through* enough—life sorts through all the people you *thought* were your friends and trims the list down to a select few you recognize as your true friends. Once you know what a friend is not, you realize the value of the friends you've got. And that's when you realize that *a true friend is a gift*.

David's Mighty Men weren't all his *close* friends; you can't have thirty-seven close friends. It's not possible. But they had a strong bond and a fierce loyalty; they were willing to die for one another. So, looking at the relationship between David and his Mighty Men, let's answer the question: What's the stuff friendships are made of? Answer: honesty, loyalty/commitment, and sacrifice. Let's look at each more closely.

Honesty

> *"Your friend is the man who knows all about you, and still likes you."* –Elbert Hubard

A true friend accepts you as you are. You know you've found a good friend when you feel no need to pretend or impress. That's not friendship; that's acting. God only made one you, so you'll never be happy trying to be somebody else! Honesty in friendship is the freedom to be yourself. It's living with nothing to hide. *This is who I am. These are my flaws. These are my strengths. This is my personality. This is what I believe. This is what I like and what I don't. What you see is what you get.*

When David and the guys who became his Mighty Men met, they all had something in common: they were outlaws! David may have been anointed to be the next king, but for eleven years he was: WANTED: DEAD OR ALIVE! And his Band of Merry Men? The Bible describes them as men who were either in some kind of trouble, owed a lot of money or were just not satisfied with life. These guys were a traveling support group: Rejects Anonymous! Maybe the reason they got so tight is that there, in that circle of friends, was the one place they were accepted just as they were. They were friends before they were famous. A true friend accepts you as you are...but challenges you to be all you can be.

I want friends who *accept me for who I am*, but I don't want friends who *won't confront me when I'm wrong* or *where I need to improve*. Sometimes my friends and I don't agree...*strongly*. Sometimes we argue...*loudly*. Sometimes my friends tell me things I don't want to hear *that I need to hear*. And I don't like it. But I'm glad they cared enough to say it anyway. I'll guarantee you David and the boys got in each other's faces a few times. In fact, knowing these guys, I'll bet some of them exchanged punches. But they pushed each other to be better men—godly men.

There's a verse in the Bible that says, *"Wounds from a friend can be trusted, but an enemy multiplies kisses."*[1] I'd rather have friends who will punch me upside the head with some tough words than a bunch of pushovers who flatter me in public but filet me in private. Another verse says, *"As iron sharpens iron, so a friend sharpens a friend."*[2] Do you have a friend who can tell you when you're wrong or that you allow to be honest with you about areas of your life where you need to improve? Don't punch him...*too* hard! That's what friends are for. And that's *the stuff friends are made of.*

Loyalty/Commitment

> *Winter, spring, summer or fall. All you have to do is call, and I'll be there.* –"You've Got a Friend" by James Taylor

> *Wealth will bring you many new friends, but become poor and your friends will leave you* (Proverbs 19:4 ERV).

> *A friend is always loyal, and a brother is born to help in time of need* (Proverbs 17:17 NLT).

The true test of friendship is hard times. You've probably heard the term "fair weather friend." The storms of life blow away fair-weather pretenders and reveal your true all-weather friends. It's both painful and powerful. *Painful* because you will be disappointed and hurt when you realize some people you thought were friends only hung around you because it benefited them some way. *Powerful* because when you see who your true friends really are, you appreciate them even more. The friends who stick by you through thick and thin are the ones with a high level of loyalty and commitment. Those two attributes mean pretty much the same thing:

Loyalty = A feeling of strong support for someone/something
Commitment = The state of being bound emotionally or intellectually to a course of action or to another person(s)

A loyal, committed friend is someone you can trust. When you're under fire, a true friend *has your back*—instead of *stabbing you in it*. When someone tells them something negative about you, they give you the benefit of the doubt, choosing to believe the best about you until they talk to you straight up. And, as I already said, a loyal, committed friend doesn't quit on you when the going gets tough. David's Mighty Men and the army that formed around him while he was living in the desert were extremely loyal to him. How do I know? Well, for one, since he had a bounty on his head, any one of them could have betrayed him to Saul for reward money or the hopes of getting in good with the king. But they didn't.

Another sign of their loyalty is the fact that they followed and fought for David for eleven years under very difficult conditions. Remember, if you joined David's team, that made *you* the king's enemy and a wanted man as well. But these guys were so loyal and committed to David that they put their lives on the line for him every day—constantly moving from place to place, hiding in the desert, living in caves, scrounging for food and water, putting their families at risk—not for a month or two, *for eleven long years.* If you can find some friends who will do that for you, you better show them some love my man, because that is major commitment! Like I said, *tough times reveal true friends.* David made some of his best friends in the desert. If a friend is loyal to you in a cave, chances are he'll have your back when you're living in a castle.

The story at the beginning of this chapter when Amasai and his men asked to join David's army is a great example of loyalty.[3] David basically said, "Look fellas. I'm a wanted man. I need to know I can trust you. If I can trust you, you're in. But if you're coming here acting like my friends so you can betray me to my enemies, God help you." And Amasai had a God moment; the Holy Spirit came on him and instantly bonded him to David for life. He said, "We are yours, David! We're with you! We're here to help you succeed. Your success is our success. We want God's best for you."[4] If you've got even *one* friend like that, you are a lucky man! You need to take him out for pizza—better yet, a steak dinner. That's a true friend. And that's *the stuff friends are made of.* One more...

Sacrifice

> *When the road looks rough ahead*
> *And you're miles and miles from your nice warm bed*
> *You just remember what your old pal said,*
> *"Boy, you've got a friend in me"*
> "You've Got a Friend in Me" by Randy Newman

There's a story about David's Mighty Men that's a great example of friends who were willing to make a *sacrifice.* You can read it for yourself in 2 Samuel 23:14-17 or 1 Chronicles 11:15-19, but here's a summary: David and his army are in one of their many battles with the Philistines. The Philistine army has set up camp in Bethlehem, which just happened to be David's hometown, the place where he grew up. Let's try to get inside David's head and heart for a minute. The enemy was camped out in his hometown. He's hot, tired, and thirsty. The man lived in constant danger and under the daily pressure of leadership responsibilities. He was probably concerned about the safety of friends and family in Bethlehem as well as the safety of his men.

I can imagine David leaning his head back against a tree or a wall, closing his eyes for a couple of minutes and daydreaming about simpler days when, as a boy, he and his buddies played in the dusty streets of Bethlehem. When they'd get really hot and thirsty, they always ran down to one particular well for a drink. The water was so cold and refreshing. And David said out loud, "Man I wish someone would get me a drink of water from the well near the gate of Bethlehem!"[5] That was it. It wasn't an order or even a serious request, just a day-dreamed wish. But that's all it took.

Three of David's Mighty Men, Jashobeam, Eleazar, and Shammah, heard him say it and decided, "Let's get David that drink of water." So they broke through enemy lines, drew water from the well, put it in a container, and carried it back to David. *They risked their lives to bring their friend a drink of water.* David was so blown away by the sacrifice of his friends that he basically said, "Fellas, I don't deserve a gift that came at such high cost." And instead of drinking it, he poured the water out as an offering to the Lord. I wonder, as David was worshipping, if he said, "And God, thank You for such amazing friends." I wonder if you've ever done that? Now's your chance. *Honesty, loyalty, and sacrifice; that's the stuff friends are made of.*

> *"I no doubt deserved my enemies, but I don't believe I deserved my friends."* –Walt Whitman

 ***In-Your-Face Challenge:***

A true friend is a gift from God. We only have a handful of truly great friends in our lifetime. Who are your true friends?

> *"It takes a long time to grow an old friend."* –John Leonard

What can you do to show them your appreciation?

"Do not save your loving speeches for your friends 'til they are dead; Do not write them on their tombstones, speak them rather now instead." –Anna Cummins

Are you as good a friend to them as they are to you?

"If all my friends were to jump off a bridge, I wouldn't jump with them; I'd be at the bottom to catch them." –Unknown

Become the Friend You Want

"He who would have friends must first show himself friendly." I not only believe that statement—I proved it. During my freshman year of college I struggled with a major identity crisis. I went from being a high school senior and "big man on campus," to a lowly college freshman—unknown and unimportant (at least it felt like it). I remember sitting in my dorm room on Friday and Saturday nights, when everyone was out having a good time, looking at myself in the mirror and just beating myself with thoughts like, *You're a nobody. You don't have any friends. You can't get a date. You're ugly. You're a loser.* It was pretty bad. So bad I almost didn't go back the next year. But I did. And when I went back, I made a very important decision that turned everything around for me.

At the beginning of my sophomore year, I decided, "I'm going to be a friend to as many people who will have me. If someone rejects me...their loss. They just missed out on a good friend." That decision changed everything for me. I made all kinds of great friends over the next three years and ended up having a blast at college. It really is true: If you want friends, then *become the kind of friend you want.* We've talked about the stuff friends are made of. So become a friend who is *honest, loyal* and willing to *sacrifice* for others. Yea, you'll get burned a time or two, but eventually, you will find some true friends.

> *"The making of friends, who are real friends, is the best token we have of a man's success in life."* –Edward Everett Hale

I Am a Friend of God

God wants to be your friend. I'm serious. The God of the universe wants to be friends with, to quote the Incredible Hulk,[6] "puny humans" like us! Abraham was called *"the friend of God."*[7] And the Bible says, *"The Lord would speak with Moses face-to-face, just as someone speaks with a friend."*[8] David wrote in amazement, *"...I wonder, "Why are people so important to You [God]? Why do you even think about them? Why do you care so much about humans?""*[9] If that's not enough evidence to convince you that God wants to be your friend, check out what Jesus said, *"I no longer call you servants, because servants don't know what their master is doing. But now I call you friends, because I have told you everything that my Father told me."*[10]

God doesn't just want to be your friend—He wants to be your *best* friend. God is *honest.* David said about Him, *"Every word you say can be trusted."*[11] He's completely *loyal: "I will never leave you; I will never abandon you."*[12] *"You can be sure that I will be with you always."*[13] You can **always** count on Him. And when it comes to *sacrifice,* no one comes close: *"The greatest love a person can show is to die for his* *friends."*[14] Do you know someone who could use a friend like that? Then I challenge you to make Jesus Christ your Best Friend, and to pray for opportunities to introduce Him to your buddies. *That's what friends are for.* If you're committed in friendship to a band of brothers, put your sword in the circle.

To Honor, To Courage, To Commitment...To God!

Sharpen your sword by memorizing this verse: *"Two people are better than one. ...If one person falls, the other can reach out to help. But those who are alone when they fall have no one to help them"* (Ecclesiastes 4:9-10 ERV).

SIN AGAINST A FRIEND

*These are the names of David's mighty men: ...Zelek...
Naharai...Ira...Gareb...and Uriah the Hittite. There were
thirty-seven in all.*

2 SAMUEL 23:8,37-39 (NIV)

*One evening David got up from his bed and walked
around on the roof of the palace...he saw a woman
bathing. The woman was very beautiful, and David
sent someone to find out about her. The man said,
"Isn't this Bathsheba...the wife of Uriah the Hittite?"
Then David sent messengers to get her. She came to
him, and he slept with her...*

2 SAMUEL 11:2-4 (NIV)

Big Idea: How to avoid sinning against a friend and
what to do if you have.

Friendly Fire

On May 31, 2002, in the aftermath of the 9/11 attacks on the United States, Pat Tillman turned down a contract offer of $3.6 million over three years from the NFL's Arizona Cardinals and instead enlisted in the United States Army along with his brother, Kevin. After participating in the invasion of Operation Iraqi Freedom, Pat entered Ranger School in September 2003 and graduated three months later on November 28. Tillman then joined the Army Rangers and served several combat tours before he died in the mountains of Afghanistan on April 22, 2004.

At first, the Army reported Tillman had been killed by enemy forces. However, following his memorial service and burial, the Department of Defense and US Congress launched investigations that eventually proved his death was the result of friendly fire; Tillman was mistakenly shot by his fellow soldiers. More than a month after he was buried, the Pentagon notified the Tillman family that their son had died from friendly fire. The family accused the Department of Defense of delaying their knowledge of the truth to protect the image of the US armed forces. Tillman was posthumously promoted from Specialist to Corporal and awarded the Silver Star and Purple Heart.

I remember hearing Pat Tillman's story and thinking, *What a sad way for a hero to die.* I felt the same way when I read the name "Uriah the Hittite" on the list of David's Mighty Men.[1] Why? Because Uriah was the husband of Bathsheba *with whom David committed adultery!* David did not (as I had always assumed) sleep with the wife of some random soldier; *he slept with the wife of a friend.* He betrayed, deceived, and murdered someone from his Circle of Swords.[2] He went behind the back of someone who had his back, and then tried to cover it up.

How could a good, godly leader do such a thing? How did he live with himself? How did he look his men in the eye? What kind of impact did David's sin against his friend have on the other members of the Circle of Swords? I pray that David's biggest mistake and the pain it caused him will stop someone who reads this chapter from making the same mistake.

Let's start by talking about...

How to Avoid Sinning Against a Friend

1. Feed the Right Fire. One of two fires is burning in you right now. The first fire I'm talking about is *the fire of the Spirit.* When you make Jesus Christ the Leader of your life, *God's Spirit,* which the Bible refers to as the *Holy Spirit,* begins to live in you, helping you recognize right from wrong and make choices that honor God. The other fire is what the Bible calls the *flesh.* The flesh is the natural, inborn desire in each of us that makes us want to sin. There's a daily battle going on inside us between these two forces or fires:

> *The sinful nature* [the flesh] *wants to do evil, which is just the opposite of what the Spirit wants. And the Spirit gives us desires that are the opposite of what the sinful nature desires. These two forces are constantly fighting each other....*[3]

The fire that burns hottest is the one you feed the most. So you need to feed the right fire.

Feeding the fire of the Spirit. The fuel that feeds God's fire in you, is *prayer, the Word of God,* and *worship.* Here's a brief description of each:

Prayer: A simple definition of prayer is *talking to and listening to God.* You can't have a good relationship with someone if you don't talk to them. It's the same with God. The problem is, guys often aren't the best communicators. God gets that; but you still have to push yourself to do it because prayer is one of the main ways you fuel the Spirit's fire. Here's some simple advice on how to pray:

1. *Talk to God like you talk to a good friend.* In the last chapter, I told you that God wants to be your friend; so talk to Him like one! Don't use fancy words or copy the way you heard someone else pray. Just be yourself. I heard of one guy who placed a chair across from him when he prayed so he could imagine having a conversation with Jesus.

2. *Be honest.* God already knows what you're thinking and feeling, so you might as well talk to Him about it. If you're ticked off, go ahead and tell God. David did. In fact, if you want help learning how to talk to God, read the Book of Psalms. You will see that whatever emotion David was feeling—anger, sadness, joy, doubt, fear—he talked about it to God. You'll never surprise God by telling Him something He doesn't *already know* or hasn't *already heard*. So be honest.

The Word of God: The Word of God is one of the ways God *talks back to us.*[4] There's information in the Bible about every subject and situation you'll ever face in life. And because the Holy Spirit helped write the Bible, it's different from any other book.[5] There's a verse that says, *"God's word is **alive** and working. It is sharper than the sharpest sword and cuts all the way into us. ...It judges the thoughts and feelings in our hearts."*[6] I challenge you to *read, listen to, memorize,* and *quote* the Word of God. And as you do, ask the Holy Spirit to bring the Word to life so it will *fuel the fire of God* in you.

Worship: Worship is *thinking about and bragging on God.* Lots of people think worship always has something to do with music, but that's just *one* of the ways to worship. Because God is everywhere and listening all the time, you can worship Him anytime, anyplace— while you're at work, driving, hunting, fishing, you name it—simply by choosing to think about and brag on Him. That's how you fuel the fire of God's Spirit in you.[7]

Now let's talk about...

Feeding the Fire of the Flesh. "*The sinful nature* [the flesh] *wants to do evil, which is just the opposite of what the Spirit wants.*"[8] The opposite of thinking *God thoughts* is thinking *sinful thoughts*. Every sin begins as a thought. The thought itself isn't necessarily a sin; but if you don't quickly recognize and replace a sinful thought with a God thought, *the sinful thought becomes fuel for the fire of the flesh.* A great example of this for us guys is sex. We're biologically wired to be turned on by sight. If you see a really good-looking woman, it doesn't take long for a *look* to become a *thought* that *lights the flame of lust.* That's what happened to David. It wasn't the first look that got him in trouble, it was the second, and the third...and in a matter of a few *seconds,* his flesh was burning with lust and he had to have Bathsheba.[9]

That's why pornography is such a big problem for guys. I'm convinced there's always a little flame of sexual interest burning in just about every man—like a "pilot light." If you fuel that fire with porn, steamy movies and music videos, etc., that little flame will erupt into a raging inferno until you find some way to satisfy the fire you started. Sexual abuse, affairs, rape, and other sexual sins are fueled by the fire of lust. I used the example of sex because so many guys can relate to that subject, but the same thing can happen with other sinful thoughts. If you constantly think about greed, jealousy, anger, hate...you're fueling the fire of the flesh.[10]

Here are two quick pieces of advice for keeping the fire of the flesh under control:

1. *Wear your night vision glasses.* Soldiers have special night vision goggles that help them see in the dark. The Spirit of God

and the Word of God are like spiritual night vision goggles that help you recognize deeds of darkness. I challenge you to put on your night vision glasses by memorizing this verse: *"...think about things that are good and worthy of praise...true and honorable and right and pure and beautiful and respected"* (Philippians 4:8 NCV). If something doesn't fit one of those descriptions, recognize it for what it is (a sinful thought) and...

2. *Fight fire with fire.* Don't just *resist* a sinful thought, *replace it* with a godly thought. If you sit around all day thinking, *I shouldn't be thinking about that hot new secretary,* then in your effort to *not* think about her, you're *reminding yourself* of her over and over! Don't tell yourself what you *won't* think about—give yourself *something better* to think about instead, like your wife, your kids, or a verse like Philippians 4:8. That's how you *fight fire with fire.*

And that's the first way to avoid sinning against a friend. You've got to feed the right fire. *"So I tell you: Live by following the Spirit. Then you will not do what your sinful selves want."*[11]

2. Practice the G-Rule. I'll never forget the first time I talked to a guy who had just learned his wife was having an affair. I was a 22-year-old rookie youth pastor. Mark[12] and his wife were newly married. They met, dated, and fell in love while attending a Christian school. They were a great couple. Until Mark found out his wife was having an affair. I felt so bad for Mark. His eyes were bloodshot. He hadn't slept for two days. He was messed up. I didn't know what to say except, "I'm so sorry." Every guy that's about to sleep with another man's wife should have to look in the face of someone like Mark and see the pain I saw that day. Believe me, you would never want something like that to happen to you. The G-Rule (Golden Rule) says, *"Do to others what you want them to do to you."*[13] Before you do something you can't undo, put yourself in the other guy's shoes—especially if that guy is a friend.

3. *Think about the RESULTS more than the RUSH.* Let's be honest: sin is fun. If it wasn't, we wouldn't do it! But the fun doesn't last. The Bible says the *"pleasures of sin"* are *"fleeting."*[14] It also says, *"...you can be sure that your sin will track you down."*[15] I have a saying that goes like this: *"The minute you sin, the bill is in the mail."* You'd better enjoy the temporary *rush* because the bill for your sin is on the way. And believe me, you're not going to want to pay! David's sin against his friend Uriah is a sad example. Not long after their fling, Bathsheba sent word to David that she was pregnant. So David had Uriah sent home from battle on a military leave of absence. His plan was for Uriah to come home, have sex with his wife, he'd think the baby was his—problem solved.

But Uriah was such a loyal soldier and friend that he refused to go home and enjoy the pleasure of his wife's company while his friends were out fighting. Instead, he slept on a mat outside David's palace. So the next day David got him drunk. But again, Uriah slept outside the palace instead of going home. When that plan failed, David sent a letter back with his friend instructing the general, *"Put Uriah on the front lines where the fighting is the worst. Then pull the troops back from him, so that he will be wounded and die."*[16] That plan worked. Uriah was killed. Bathsheba moved into the palace. And David thought he had pulled it off. But he didn't.

There's another verse in the Bible that goes like this: *"What you have said in the dark will be heard in the daylight. What you have whispered to someone behind closed doors will be shouted from the rooftops."*[17] David learned the hard way that there's no such thing as a secret. God told David's secret to Nathan the prophet. Nathan confronted David. And the *rush* of his one-night-stand gave way to the painful *results* of his sin. David lost his infant son, he had to live with the guilt of what he did to his friend, he had to look his Mighty Men in the eye and admit that he had betrayed and murdered one of his inner circle. (I wonder how that conversation went?) Worst of all,

David's close relationship with God was disrupted and he agonized over it.

In-Your-Face Challenge:

If you're planning and dreaming about some secret sin, I pray you stop right now and think past the *rush* to the *results*. Think of what it's going to feel like when your wife, your kids, your friends, the people at your church find out. Think of what it's going to cost you. Think about the people it's going to affect. Think about what it's going to do to your relationship with God. And DON'T DO IT! The rush will never be worth the pain.

4. *Get in and Stay in a Circle of Swords.* All those years when he was running for his life from Saul, David stayed solid in his relationship with God. In hard times and places, he built an army of men so loyal they were willing to die for him and forged friendships that lasted a lifetime. But at the time of his greatest failure, we read: *"...at the time of year when kings usually go to war, David sent out Joab with his officers and the Israelite army...but David himself stayed in Jerusalem."*[18] David's not living in caves anymore; he's living in a castle. He's no longer an outlaw; he's the king of Israel. And he's no longer wearing his sword taking on the enemy; he's sitting home alone, all by himself. Boredom made him vulnerable to the enemy in a different kind of way.

David recognized the enemy *on the battlefield*. But he failed to recognize the enemy *from his balcony*. If David had stayed engaged in battle alongside his Mighty Men, he would never have sinned against his friend. Are you getting this? Satan doesn't care how he takes down a man of God; he just wants him down. If you've made Jesus Christ the Leader of your life, *you need to be in a Circle of Swords.* You need a group of godly friends who can look you in the eye and ask the hard questions like: *"Where have you been? What have you been doing and who have you been doing it with? How's your marriage? Are you spending too much time at work and not enough at home? Is there compromise in your life? Are you lying to me?"*

That's called *accountability.* And that's what David had when he was hanging with his bros in the cave. But that's what he was missing when he walked out on his balcony all alone. If you are living in isolation with no one to hold you accountable, you're asking for trouble. Find some guys who are God chasers and form a Circle of Swords.

That's *How to Keep From Sinning Against a Friend.* I hope you'll take that advice and do everything you can to avoid the pain that always comes with sin. Many guys who read this book may have already stepped across that line. If you're living with the fallout of a sinful decision, or you know a friend who is, this next section is for you.

Making Things Right (The Psalm 51 Model)

David was such a great example of godly character up until his sin with Bathsheba. I wish (like I'm sure he did many times) he had never compromised himself and his reputation; but he did. To his credit, as I said in Chapter 1, even when David fell and fell hard, he never stopped chasing God. So, although I wish he had never sinned, I'm thankful we can read David's words as he wrote about his agonizing journey through and eventually up and out of that dark time in his life. Psalm 51, which David wrote right after his "pastor" (Nathan the prophet) confronted him about his sin with Bathsheba, is a model for making things right when we have sinned.

If that's where you find yourself right now, I encourage you to do what David did:

1. Come Clean (Repent) *(Psalm 51:3-6). "I know I have done wrong,"* with those words, David came clean. Repentance is more than feeling bad because you got caught; it is *admitting* you did the wrong thing, *taking responsibility* for your actions, being *genuinely sorry* for what you've done, and *being willing to do* whatever God asks you to do to make things right. That's not easy. Your pride will fight against it. When David was confronted for his sin, he could have said, *"Hey, I'm the king, I can do whatever I want."* Instead, he wrote: *"The sacrifice God wants is a broken spirit. God, you will not reject a heart that is broken and sorry for sin."*[19] He humbly came clean **to God:** *"I did what you said is wrong. You are the one I have sinned against. I say this so that people will know that I am wrong and you are right."*[20]

I've heard many people say, "My sin isn't hurting anyone...." That's a lie. Sin *always* hurts someone—starting with God. In the previous chapter I told you God wants to be your friend. God is the first and most important friend you hurt when you sin. So you need to start by making things right with Him. Use David's words, *"God, I did the wrong thing and I hurt you. I blew it and I know it. Please forgive me..."* No hiding. No excuses.

Once you come clean with God, you need to come clean **to the person you sinned against:** *"I remember that sin all the time. My sin is always before me."*[21] Many times, people apologize to God for their sin, but fail to apologize to the people they sinned against. The Bible actually says in several places that our relationship with God can't be right until our relationship with those we sinned against is made right.[22]

Unfortunately for David, the friend he sinned against (Uriah) was dead. But there were still people he needed to come clean to:

Bathsheba, Nathan his "Pastor," Uriah's family, and the Mighty Men in his Circle of Swords. David's sin disrupted the unity in his band of brothers. He betrayed one of his own. There's no record of it, but I believe there had to be a moment when David squared up with his men and said, "Fellas, I did a terrible thing...." I don't know how they could have continued to fight for him, respect him—or feel safe that he wouldn't do to them what he did to Uriah—if David didn't come clean with his men.

 *In-Your-Face Challenge:*

Who has your sin hurt?

Who makes up the community that's been affected by what you've done?

If you've sinned against a friend and you want closure, it's time to man up and come clean with your family, your friends, your church leadership, your co-workers—whoever the Holy Spirit tells you to. If you're not sure, pray and God will show you.

2. Receive Forgiveness (Psalm 51:1-2; 7-9 ERV). "God, be merciful to me because of your unfailing love...erase all the wrongs I have done. Scrub away my guilt. Wash me clean from my sin. Wash me until I am whiter than snow! Let me hear sounds of joy and happiness again. Don't look at my sins. Erase them all." Like I said, I'm sorry David sinned. But I'm really thankful I can read the words he used when he asked God to forgive Him. You can feel his emotion and regret and his desire to have his relationship with God restored. God felt and saw it and forgave David the instant he came clean: *"David said to Nathan, 'I have sinned against the Lord.' Nathan replied, 'The Lord has taken away your sin.'"*[23]

God will do the same for you. One of my favorite verses in the Bible says, *"If we confess our sins to God, he can always be trusted to forgive us and take our sins away."*[24] God is ready to forgive us the instant we get honest with Him. My friend, God still loves you! He still wants a relationship with you! If you've not done it yet, stop right now to thank God and accept His forgiveness.

3. *Submit to Restoration* *(Psalm 51:10-12 ERV). "Create a pure heart in me, and make my spirit strong again. Don't push me away or take your Holy Spirit from me. Your help made me so happy. Give me that joy again. Make my spirit strong and ready to obey you."* Receiving forgiveness is the good part of coming clean. But God loves us too much to just let us go right back to life business as usual. Your willingness to submit to restoration is very important—to you and to God—and will have huge implications on your future moving forward past the place of your sin.

There are two important differences between *forgiveness* and *restoration* that you need to understand and prepare for, or I guarantee that you will get frustrated and be tempted to bail out on the process.

First, *God's forgiveness is instantaneous, but restoration takes time.* Restoration isn't a moment or a day or a week or a month, it's a process. How long? The length of time varies. A good answer: as long as it takes you to work, talk, and pray your way through your mistake and get healthy. And not by your own evaluation, by the evaluation of trusted godly mentors and leaders. In some cases, they will come to you and offer; or in cases of church discipline, even require you to submit to a restoration process. If no one comes to you, then you go to them. Talk to your pastor and ask him and your church leadership to give you a restoration plan and provide you with spiritual mentors who can walk with you through that plan. We all want quick fixes; but if you don't learn from your mistakes, you often repeat them. So be patient and submit yourself to God, godly mentors and friends.

Second, *forgiveness immediately erases the guilt of sin, but restoration helps you deal with the consequences that always follow sin.* Remember how I said, the minute you sin, the bill is in the mail? Well, unfortunately, it won't take long before the bills start to arrive. And like any bills, you aren't going to like paying them. Don't get mad at God. The bills aren't His fault! He hates to see us in pain. That's why He warns us *"...you can be sure that your sin will track you down."*[25] And don't get mad at or blame others. As I said in the previous section, take responsibility for your actions, learn from your mistake, take your lumps, and pray your way through this time period with the help of a Circle of Swords (some good Christian friends).

Read this carefully: If you receive God's forgiveness for your sin but take shortcuts on the restoration process, you haven't learned all you needed to learn and you are very likely to repeat the same mistake(s). *Forgiveness* and *restoration* aren't the same thing. One without the other is a shortcut to *making things right* with God. Go all the way and put it behind you once and for all.

4. Stay Humble and Thank God *(Psalm 51:13-17). "Then I will teach your ways to those who do wrong, and sinners will turn back to you...and I will sing about your goodness. Lord, let me speak so I may praise you."* I agree with Rick Warren when he says, "God never

79

wastes a hurt." If you will do the things we just talked about—*come clean, receive forgiveness* and *submit to restoration*—God will not only bring you through the dark days caused by your sin, He will use your mistakes and the things you learned, to help others. *How?* As you tell the story of your painful journey, God may use you to stop someone before they make the same mistake. And for guys who have fallen into sin, you will be a great mentor to help them get back up because you know what it's like to be in their shoes! Our greatest ministry often comes out of our deepest pain. If you stay humble and continue to thank God every day for forgiving and restoring you, He will use you.

David and his Mighty Men were far from perfect. They were just like you and me. We all fail the Lord. We all sin. A Circle of Swords isn't made up of perfect men—it's made up of men who are honest about their mistakes. If you are committed to God to help you avoid sinning against a friend, and promise to be honest with Him even when you fail, put your sword in the circle.

To Honor, To Courage, To Commitment...To God!

Sharpen your sword by memorizing these two verses: *"...you may be sure that your sin will find you out"* (Numbers 32:23 NLT). *"What you have said in the dark will be heard in the daylight. What you have whispered to someone behind closed doors will be shouted from the rooftops"* (Luke 12:3 New International Reader's Version).

CHAPTER 8

FIGHT FOR YOUR FAMILY

By the time David and his men came to the town, it had been burned down, and their wives, sons, and daughters had been taken captive.

1 SAMUEL 30:3 (GOD'S WORD TRANSLATION)

David fought them from dusk until the evening of the next day, and...recovered everything the Amalekites had taken...

1 SAMUEL 30:17-18 (NIV)

...Don't be afraid...Remember the Lord who is great and awesome, and fight for your brothers, your sons and your daughters, your wives and your homes.

NEHEMIAH 4:14 (NIV)

Big Idea: God is ready to help you fight against enemy forces that want to destroy your family.

In 1 Samuel chapter 30 there's a story about David and his men that impacts me every time I read it. Tired of constantly running for his life from Saul, David along with his six hundred men and their families, were given permission to live in the Philistine city of Ziklag. When Saul heard David was living in enemy territory, he stopped chasing him. For a year and four months, David and his men lived among the Philistines, leading raiding parties against the common enemies of the Philistines and the Israelites, and gaining the trust of the leader of that area, King Achish. Achish came to trust David so much that when the combined forces of the Philistines gathered for war, he allowed David and his men to join them!

Well, Achish may have trusted David, but the Philistine commanders *did not!* When they heard that "the Giant killer" was among their ranks, they made Achish send David and his men back to Ziklag for fear that they would turn on them in the heat of battle. David protested, but early the next morning, he and his men started the three-day journey home.[1] Here's where the story gets interesting. On the third day they came within view of their homes. And, *"When David and his men came to Ziklag, they found the city burning. Their wives, sons, and daughters were all gone. The Amalekites had taken them."*[2]

Appreciate What You Have

"David and the men in his army cried loudly until they were too weak to cry anymore."[3]

Put yourself in their place and try to imagine how David and his men felt when they saw smoke from their city rising in the distance. They instantly knew something was wrong. Their hearts started racing and, even though they were tired from walking for three days straight, adrenaline kicked in and they started running. As they got closer, they could see that their homes were destroyed and every man was thinking the same thing, *Is my family dead?* Frantically, they began digging through the charred ashes of their homes, calling out the names of their wives, their sons and their daughters—and looking for their remains. The good news, they found no bodies. The bad news, all of their family members were gone; taken captive by the enemy.

And 600 grown men began, one-by-one, to fall to the ground...and cry. There were no hands to hold. No smiling faces to greet them. No laughter. No little voices shouting, "Daddy's home!" The only sound echoing through the empty streets of the city was the sound of men weeping for their families. As a pastor, more than once I've had to break the news to family members that their loved one unexpectedly died. I've seen people drop to their knees in shock, crying out uncontrollably from grief. As a husband and father of three, thinking about all those men crying out for their families puts a lump in my throat.

And their story reminds me that we often don't appreciate what we have *until it's gone*. Death instantly makes us aware of things we took for granted. And it leaves us wishing for "one mores"—one more hug, one more kiss, one more conversation, one more day. But sadly, we realize that the things we thought we could do *any day*, and the things we kept putting off *until tomorrow*, we will never have the chance to do again.

 ***In-Your-Face Challenge:***

If your family was suddenly, tragically taken from you, what would you wish you could have another opportunity to say to them? Write those things down here:

Now, plan a time to say those things today or this week. Don't put it off!

What are the "one mores" you would wish you could still do with them? List those things here:

Now, take your list and begin to plug those ideas into your schedule.

Don't put off until tomorrow things you would wish you had done today!

Stay Close to God

> *David was desperate. His soldiers were so upset over what had happened to their sons and daughters that they were thinking about stoning David to death.[4] But David found strength in the Lord his God.[5]*

David was in a bad place. Not only was he grieving the loss of his own family; but he had 600 men, whose grief quickly turned to anger, thinking about killing him for leading them away into a battle that wasn't even theirs to fight, leaving their families exposed to enemy raiders. These guys were boiling over with emotion and they were looking for someone or something to take it out on. And David is the one who made the decision that took them away from their families.

David was overcome with guilt, grief, stress, fear. As the leader, he felt responsible for what happened. I can imagine him saying to himself, *This is all my fault. I should have never led my men into that fight. We may never see our families again. How can I live with myself?*

Satan, who Jesus said lives to *"steal and kill and destroy"* would love to get you, as a husband and a father, so busy and distracted fighting someone else's battles that you neglect your own family. Every day men put less-important priorities ahead of the most valuable people in their lives. Don't miss this: If you're gone too long, if you miss too much, if you put all your time and energy into your job, you're liable to come home one day and find that while you were away, Satan came in and stole your family! He's looking for a way *right now* to ruin your marriage, separate you (physically and emotionally) from your children, and steal your most valuable treasure—your family.

Maybe it has already happened and you find yourself, like David, sitting around with regrets, grieving your loss and blaming yourself. *Maybe you still have your family, but this chapter is a wake-up call* and you're suddenly realizing that your priorities are way out of line and it honestly scares you. Wherever you find yourself spiritually, emotionally, and relationally regarding your family, I encourage you to do what David did: *"find strength in the Lord."* The two versions of the Bible I used actually say, *"David was **desperate**. [So he] found strength in the Lord."*

When a man gets desperate before God, it *always* gets God's attention! Even the man who says, "I don't know how to pray" learns to pray when he's desperate! What do you think David's prayer was like? How does a desperate husband and father, pray? *"God help me! My heart feels like it's been ripped out of my chest! My wife and babies are missing! My men are talking about killing me...and I don't blame them. I feel responsible for what has happened. What should I do God? Should I go after them? Can we get our families back?"* It's time for men to get *desperate* for their families! Desperate to allow God to change their hearts and their habits and their schedules...whatever needs to change. If you will get, and stay desperate, *God will get involved!*

God told David, *"Pursue them....*[6] *You will catch them, and you will save your families."*[7] That's powerful! God wants you to pursue your family! But there's more. *"David and the six hundred men with him came to Besor Valley, where some stayed behind. Two hundred were too exhausted to cross the valley, but David and the other four hundred continued the pursuit."*[8] These guys didn't just chase after their families, they pursued them to the point of exhaustion! That's how bad they wanted them back. The question is: how can a man love his family that much and keep them his highest priority? And the answer: you can't do it on your own! *"David found strength in the Lord his God."* Only *God* can give you the strength, courage, and conviction every day to be the husband and father that your family deserves you to be! And God wants to help you fight for your family.

Fight for your Family!

> *David* [and his men] *fought the Amalekites from dusk until the evening of the next day...*[9]

The Bible doesn't say how many days it took, but David and his Mighty Men continued the desperate search for their families until they finally found them. Can you imagine the emotion they felt when they saw that enemy camp? Perhaps from their hiding place they could see their wives and children sitting on the ground with their hands tied or heavily guarded in some kind of makeshift corral. And *the blood of 400 men began to boil* as they saw their families being held captive. They were ready to rip off some heads! That's how I would have felt!

I remember years ago sitting beside my friend Jamie Kjos as our bus pulled out of the church parking lot on our way to the airport for a missions trip. As I looked out the window at my wife and three small children waving goodbye to me, I felt so much emotion, and I said to Jamie, "That's my whole life right there." I imagine David and his Mighty Men were thinking and feeling the same thing as they saw their families, huddled in scared little groups inside the enemy camp. All they could think about in that moment, *all that mattered in the world was getting their families back.* They were ready to fight and even die for their families.

That's the way we should live *every day.* So let me give you some motivation; *the enemy wants to steal your family!* He wants your kids on drugs. He wants you to lose them in a drunk driving accident after a Friday night party. He wants your daughter's virginity. He wants your son to commit suicide. He wants to create an emotional wedge between you and your kids so you stop talking, except to say hurtful things each other. *The enemy wants your kids. Satan also wants to destroy your marriage.* He wants you to neglect and walk out on the woman you promised to love and to cherish until one of you dies. He wants you to get hooked on porn or to climb in bed with another woman. He wants you to get so distracted with money and power and the pleasures this world offers that you forget that *your family **is** your world.*

Are you going to let that happen? Are you the man of the house? Then ***fight for your family!*** You may be reading this thinking, *But I've already lost them....* It's never too late to pursue your family! If you pray and ask God, He will tell you every time, *"Go after them. Pursue them until you're exhausted—and then pursue them some more."* And if you humbly ask, God will help you pursue your family. I cannot guarantee you that God will give your family or your marriage back the way it was before the enemy came in and tried to steal them away, but I *can* tell you every wife and every son and daughter on the planet wants a man (husband, father) who loves them enough to fight for them! *"Greater love has no man than this: to lay down his life for his family."*[10]

And I can also guarantee you that *God will make you the best man—* and the best husband, father, son and brother—*you can be.* You may have trouble seeing yourself this way, but *God wants you to be a holy warrior* standing at the front door of your home, ready to defend it against invisible, demonic forces. If you don't believe me, read this:

> *...I tell you, be strong in the Lord and in His great power. ...We are fighting against the spiritual powers of evil... That is why you need to get God's full armor. Then on the day of evil, you will be able to stand strong.*[11]

 ***In-Your-Face Challenge:***

Are you ready to fight for your family? In what ways do you need to fight for or guard your marriage? (Maybe you need to change your schedule, go for counseling, get an Internet filter that blocks porn, apologize...whatever you need to do, DO IT!)

What are the battles you need to fight for your children? (Talk to them and find out what they are feeling and facing, their fears and challenges. Then begin to pray about those things every day.)

Don't Give Up!

David fought them from dusk until the evening of the next day, and...recovered everything the [enemy] *had taken....*[12]

David and his 400 exhausted men fought for their families for most of twenty four hours straight. And that was after a three-day march home from war and however many days it took to find the enemy camp. I'm sure there were many times when their bodies and their logical minds were screaming, "IT'S HOPELESS!" But they refused to give up. And you could ask any of them, after they were finally reunited and could hold their wives and kids in their arms again, and they would tell you, *"It was worth all the struggle and the pain to get my family back!"* God can restore what the enemy has stolen!

You may be at the point of giving up. You've been in a fight—not just for days, but maybe for years. Maybe it's against your son or daughter's addiction. Maybe you've been fighting for your marriage for what seems like forever—seeing counselor after counselor. You're not just tired; you're exhausted. And your logical mind is telling you, *It's hopeless. Give up the fight.* I understand. And I empathize with your pain and struggle. But don't drop your sword. And don't give up! Because our God is a restorer of stolen property! Ask Him for strength *right now* and give it one more push. *It will be worth all the struggle and the pain to see God break through in your family!*

If you've made a commitment to let God transform you into a holy warrior who's willing to fight for your family, put your sword in the circle.

To Honor, To Courage, To Commitment...To God!

Sharpen your sword by memorizing this verse: *"Don't be afraid... Remember the Lord who is great and awesome, and fight for your brothers, your sons and your daughters, your wives and your homes"* (Nehemiah 4:14).

CHAPTER 9

CAMPFIRE STORIES

I wonder why you care, God—why do you bother with us at all? All we are is a puff of air; we're like shadows in a campfire.

PSALM 144:3-4 (MSG)

Generation after generation stands in awe of your work [God]; each one tells stories of your mighty acts.

PSALM 145:4 (MSG)

Let the redeemed of the Lord tell their story...

PSALM 107:2 (NIV)

Big Idea: When you come to the end of the journey, what stories will they tell about you?

I've Got One Better Than That!

Most guys have spent time around a campfire at some point in their lives. Besides the obvious benefits of keeping warm, roasting a hot dog, or heating up a pot of coffee, a campfire is a great place for friends to connect, laugh, and tell stories. Many times we tell the same stories we've told dozens of times before—but we tell 'em again anyway. Stories reliving the "glory days" of our athletic past *(The older I get, the greater I was.).* Stories of great hunting and fishing adventures *(You think THAT was a big bass, let tell you about the time...).* And there are usually a few crazy stories of the ridiculously stupid things we did when we were teenagers and young adults (or just last week...) that we were lucky to survive—or not get caught! You get me started telling stories and I can go all night. Here are a few of my favorites. See if you can top these campfire stories:

Man Down!

At the annual Woodward Elks Rodeo, some of our high school classmates bet me and my best friend we wouldn't tip over a porta-john...*with someone in it.* We were more than up for the challenge. Our victim was a big cowboy with a white Stetson hat. We waited until he settled in and got comfortable and then attacked, pushing the porta-john over on the door so he couldn't get out. I can still hear him yelling, "Hey! Hey! Heeeeyyyy!" The rest of the night, we were on the lookout for a big cowboy with a stained Stetson.

Wayne and the Tennis Ball

I was kinda' mean to my younger brother when we were growing up. (He says I was *really* mean. What a baby...) Not sure why I was mean to him. It just seemed like my duty. I talked him into sticking his finger in a hot cigarette lighter once. "C'mon man," I told him, "it will feel good." *It didn't.* It left little burn rings on his finger. Then there was the time I talked him into letting me shoot him in the butt with our Daisy BB gun. It was so weak I convinced him it couldn't possibly hurt. *It did.* One day Wayne was tight-rope walking across the top of the wooden fence in our backyard. So I threw a rock, hit him in the head, and knocked him off! But my favorite story involves me, my brother, and a tennis ball...

It was late evening and we were in my neighbor's front yard, bouncing a tennis ball off their red brick fireplace. Suddenly, without warning, I felt the urge to throw the tennis ball as hard as I could at my brother, who was standing just a few feet away from me. Sensing he was once again my target, Wayne started to let out a scream as I let 'er rip high and hard! It was dark enough that I wasn't sure what happened to the tennis ball...until I heard my brother grunting and pointing frantically at his mouth! I know you're not going to believe me, but as Wayne was yelling, "Nooo!" that tennis ball popped into his mouth, forcing his jaws wide open! I had to press in on the ball, turn it sideways, and pull it out. Wayne immediately yelled, "My jaws, my jaws!" Fortunately, he was all right, and he and I had a story we've told many times...

I Caught a Bird!

Every summer my family took a two-week vacation to the Rocky Mountains about thirty miles from Taos, New Mexico. When we got older, my brother and I joined Dad and we would catch hundreds of trout in the stream that ran behind the cabins and through the valley. But when we were younger, Dad would go fishing without us (because if he took us with him, we would throw rocks in the stream and scare the fish, or someone would come back bleeding...). So, one day, being the great lady she is, Mom took Wayne and me down the road a ways to a little pond to fish. After a while (I think about two minutes), we were bored stiff.

So I hooked a huge bass plug called a River Runt on my line and started zinging it across the pond. After one particular cast, I saw a bird that was flying over the pond take an instant nose dive into the water. I thought, *That's weird!* Then as I was reeling in, I noticed the bird was getting closer...and closer. That's when I realized, "Hey, Mom...Wayne...I caught a bird!" I brought the bird to shore and would you believe there was not a hook in it? I had lassoed the bird in mid-flight! What are the odds of that!? Am I good or what! We dried out the little fella and he flew off. Good as new! (Except for the bad dreams when it woke up screaming in the middle of the night...)

One more...

Put Eet on My Back

One of my best friends is Steve Baillargeon. Steve is French-Canadian, a logger by trade and the greatest outdoorsman I've ever met. We've been on some unforgettable hunting and fishing adventures together. Steve's garage, where all his big buck mounts are on display, looks like a Bass Pro Shop or Cabela's. When I first met Steve, he barely spoke English and many of his sentences featured the f-bomb (the first word he learned in English). I could tell you more stories about Steve than I have room to write, but here's one of my favorites.

Steve, my buddy Ray Deremer and his son Cody, and I had been hunting all day. We had three deer down, it was getting dark and we had a six-mile walk up and over the mountain back to our vehicles. (Steve never does anything the easy way.) I knew that once we got *Ray's deer* out on the carrying cart, Steve and I still had another four-mile walk back (one way) to get *our* two deer. We had only gone about a mile when we heard a loud CRACK after pulling the cart over a fallen tree. One of the wheels on the carrier had broken. We would have to drag the deer the remaining five miles. What a *drag*...

Then Steve said in his thick French-Canadian accent, "Put eet on my back and I'll carry eet." We protested, "That's crazy," but he insisted. So Ray and I lifted a field-dressed deer onto his shoulders—probably 120 pounds of dead weight flopping around—and Steve started walking up the mountain. Steve is not a big man, 6 feet tall and slightly over 180 pounds, but he's deceptively strong (obviously). He only stopped twice for a break. Then we reloaded the deer on his shoulders, and off he'd go again. I remember Ray and I, huffing and puffing just from carrying guns and backpacks, looking at each other in absolute disbelief. It was almost superhuman. Steve carried that deer to the top of the mountain, and from there, with gravity on our side, we took turns dragging it down. I'll never forget it.

Tales of the Circle of Swords

I'm sure David and his Mighty Men sat around telling campfire stories. Stories about women and war, stories about practical jokes they played on each other, stories of narrow escapes from King Saul and his bounty hunters. But some of their favorite stories had to be the ones that made it into the pages of the Bible. Like the stories of King Arthur and his Knights of the Round Table, the Tales of the Circle of Swords were the stuff of legend.

I imagine David's top three leaders, Jashobeam, Eleazar, and Shammah (*Josh, Zar,* and *Shammy*), were competitive; always trying to outdo one another, even in their storytelling. As someone who has sat around campfires with "real men," I can imagine a campfire conversation like this...

Shammy: *"Hey fellas, remember the time we were fighting the Philistines in that field of lentils and everyone ran off and left me and I had to whip their butts all by myself?!"*[1]

Zar: *"Aww Shammy, quit your whinin'. David and me called out a bunch of Phillys down at Pas Dammim and the same thing happened to us! Everyone ran away but us. I cut down so many Phillys that day that my hand cramped up and froze to my sword. You guys had to pry it open. Remember?"*[2]

Shammy: *"Yeah, he couldn't wipe his butt for a week!"* (laughter)

Zar: *"That's why I had you wipe it for me!"* (laughter)

Shammy: *"I'm gonna' come over there and KICK your butt!"* (more laughter)

Zar: *"I'd like to see you try!"* (Shammy and Zar start wrestling...Josh intervenes)

Josh: *"All right boys, break it up. I got one thing to say..."* (pause for effect) *"eight hundred..."*

Zar: *"Oh, here we go..."*

Josh: *"When you guys kill eight hundred Phillys in one battle, come talk to me."*[3]

Shammy: *"Yeah, yeah...I heard it was more like three hundred.*[4] *You never were good at math.* (mocking Josh with his "dumby" voice) *"Duh, hey Zar, What's a hundred-and-fifty plus a hundred-and-fifty?"* (pause for effect) *"Eight hundred!"* (laughter)

Zar: *"How about the time the three of us broke through enemy lines to get David a drink of water from his favorite well in Bethlehem?"*[5]

Josh: *"Yeah, how about that David?! Tell everyone what you did with the water we risked our necks for!"*

David: *"I poured it out..."* (Josh cuts him off mid-sentence)

Josh: (mimicking David) *"I'd sure like a drink of water from my favorite well in Bethlehem...so I could POUR IT OUT ON THE GROUND after my buddies risk their lives for it."* (laughter)

David (sarcastically): *"You're so funny Josh! You know that's not the way it went down. By the way, you're not the only guy who took on an army by himself. What about the day Abishai took out three hundred Phillys with nothing but a spear?"*[6]

Josh: *"Yeah, not bad...less than HALF the amount I killed in a day."*

Shammy: *"There goes Mr. Math Whiz again!"* (laughter)

David: *"Well if you ask me, Benni's got you ALL beat!"* (someone in the back yells, *"Teacher's Pet!"* and everyone laughs again) *"I'm just sayin' I'd put Benni up against anyone. He took out those two Moabite super-soldiers, snatched that giant Egyptian's spear right out of his hands and killed him with it, and when I dared everyone to go down into a pit with a lion, Benni's the only guy who had the guts to do it! And it was snowing!"*[7]

Josh: *"He got lucky."* (Josh does a demonstration of Benni slipping and sliding around until he "accidentally" stabs the lion) *"Whoa...whoa...hey look! I killed the lion!"* (loud laughter)

And on they would go late into the night...

What are some of the favorite stories you and your buddies tell when you get together?

God Stories

I'm a storyteller. Over the years, I've filed away quite a collection. I like all kinds of stories: funny stories, stories of adventure, stories of overcoming the odds. But my favorite stories are God stories—the kind that prove God is real and that He wants to be involved in our brief, ordinary lives. Stories like the one about an unknown shepherd boy who God knew was a giant killer and a king. Stories about a bunch of outlaws and rejects who became a great army *"like the army of God."*[8] Stories like the day a French-Canadian logger showed up (very reluctantly) for church, felt the Holy Spirit talking to him, eventually gave his life to Jesus, and became one of my best friends. Stories of triumph, hope, healing, forgiveness, and reconciliation.

God stories about...

- addicts and alcoholics who got clean.
- prisoners who found freedom while they were still in jail.
- husbands and fathers who won their wives and families back.
- prideful men who humbled themselves before it was too late.
- broken men who found hope in the Lord.

Stories of old men and young men, white men and black men, rich men and poor men, good men and evil men who became God's Men! *Mighty Men of God!* And *you've got a story to tell!* The Bible says, *"Let the redeemed of the Lord tell their story..."*[9] Your story is unique, one-of-a-kind. And it's not over yet. Maybe the beginning or the middle of your story wasn't so great—but the final chapters have yet to be written! Stop right here and let me get in your face one last time.

In-Your-Face Challenge:

If your life were over today, would you be proud of the story of your life? If not, what are you going to do about it? (I often say, "Live your life in such a way that when it's time for your funeral, you made the preacher's job easy!")

What kind of stories do you want God to help you write from here on?

Can I give you some advice? *Get busy* letting God help you write the remaining chapters of your life, because sooner than you realize, your story will come to an end. The Bible talks a lot about how quickly our lives go by in verses like this: *"I wonder why you care, God—why do you bother with us at all? All we are is a puff of air; we're like shadows in a campfire."* [10] God still has some great adventures planned for you! Are you up for it? The stories we tell at the end of our lives will be the sum of the adventures we chose to live on the journey. Jesus promised: *"I came so they can have real and eternal life, more and better life than they ever dreamed of!"* [11] So take Him up on His offer and live your one-and-only life to the *max* for God!

And when you reach the end of your journey and your friends and family gather to tell their campfire stories about you, may they tell true tales of a man who chose to *follow **the** Leader*. A man of character whose *name and reputation* were respected by all who knew him. A man who often got away from it all to *hide out with God*. A *brave-hearted man* who *used his God-given skills* to make a difference in this hurting world. A man who was *a true friend*. A husband and father who *fought for his family*.

I guarantee you, if that's the story of your life, Mighty Man of God... *you will be somebody's hero*. And maybe when you get to heaven, some guy standing with a bunch of rough-looking dudes will call you over, hand you a sword and say, *"We've been waiting for you. Put your sword in the circle..."*

To Honor, To Courage, To Commitment...To God!

Sharpen your sword one last time by memorizing this verse: *"Generation after generation stands in awe of your work* [God]; *each one tells stories of your mighty acts"* (Psalm 145:4 MSG).

APPENDIX A

MAKING JESUS CHRIST THE LEADER OF YOUR LIFE (HOW TO START A RELATIONSHIP WITH GOD)

There are just three simple steps to making Jesus Christ the leader of your life:

STEP ONE: *Admit* you're a sinner. The Bible makes it clear that we *all* have a sin problem: *"**Everyone** has sinned; **we all fall short** of God's...standard."*[1] You're not a *worse sinner* than someone else; and you're not *less-of-a-sinner* than someone else. You're just *a sinner,* period. The Bible doesn't compare you to anyone but God—who's perfect. So when we *admit we're sinners,* we're simply agreeing, "God's perfect, and I'm not. I can't live up to His standards." Although that's true for everyone, it's still hard to admit because of pride. That's why a relationship with God starts by humbling yourself and admitting, "I'm a sinner."

STEP TWO: *Believe* that Jesus paid the price for sin. People believe there are many ways to be accepted by God and granted access to heaven when we die. But the Bible gives only one way: Believe in Jesus Christ. Not just that He *existed.* Believe that *He was and is the Son of God,* that *He lived a sinless life,* and that when He willingly gave His perfect life on the cross, *God accepted His sacrifice as the only payment for our sins.* John 3:16 says, *"God loved the world so much that he gave his one and only Son, so that **everyone who believes in him will not perish but have eternal life.**"* The second step to a relationship with God is believing what the Bible says about who Jesus is and accepting what He did on the cross as God's only solution to the problem of sin.

101

STEP THREE: *Confess* with words that come from your mouth and your heart and ask Jesus Christ to be the Lord of your life. I often say, "A belief is not really a belief until you're willing to *live it*." Thousands of people will tell you, "Yea, I believe in Jesus" if you ask them. But many of them don't know God and they aren't going to heaven. Why? Because it's not enough to believe; you've got to *act* on what you believe. That's why this last step is so important. Acting on your belief, you say, "God, not only do I *believe* in Jesus, *I choose Jesus* to be the Leader and Lord of my life." Romans 10:9 says, *"You will be saved, **if you honestly say**, 'Jesus is Lord,' and if you **believe with all your heart** that God raised him from death."*

The following prayer contains the three steps necessary to make Jesus Christ the Leader and Lord of your life. Are you ready? God has been waiting for this moment from the time you were born. He's listening right now as you pray...

> *God, I admit I'm a sinner. Thanks for loving me anyway. I believe in Jesus. I believe He's Your Son. And I believe that when He gave His sinless life on the cross, it took care of my sin problem. Not only do I **believe** in Jesus; I **want** Him to be the Leader of my life. Come into my life, Jesus. Help me live for God. In Jesus' name. Amen.*

Congratulations on your decision to follow Christ! I wish I was there with you to celebrate. Your new life with God as your Leader has just begun. Let me stress: THIS IS JUST THE BEGINNING. God will be working on you for the rest of your life; helping you live more like Jesus. There's a bumper sticker that says, *Christians aren't perfect; they're just forgiven.* It's true! Don't get frustrated or think Jesus cut you from the team the first time you make a mistake. Just be honest with God when you sin, ask Him to forgive you right away, and move forward. God is committed to you and He will help you grow stronger through each challenge.

This last part is very important: Now that you've asked Jesus to be the Leader of your life, you need to find a guy who's been serving God for a while, tell him about your decision, and ask if you can hang out with him at least once a week for the next two or three months. Tell him, *"I want to learn everything I can about how to live for God—how to pray, how to read the Bible. I need someone who can help answer questions about things I don't understand. Will you disciple me?"*[2] I can't stress how important that is! Many Christians never learn the basics of following Christ. As a result, they never discover and become all God intended for them, or they back out on their commitment completely. Discipleship is so important that it was one of final commands Jesus gave to all believers before He left earth.[3] You will *never forget* the person who disciples you! Don't put this off. Pray about it and ask God to direct you to someone right away!

APPENDIX B
PLANNING A SPIRITUAL/LIFE-FOCUS RETREAT
(A GETAWAY WITH GOD)

Here are some starter ideas to help you have a successful retreat. Feel free to adapt or add to them as you like.

Rest...from your hectic schedule/routine

Relax

On a scale of 1-10, how would you rate your stress level?

Low				Moderate				High	
1	2	3	4	5	6	7	8	9	10

Here are a few ideas to help you relax during your time away:

_____ Disconnect from the outside world by giving yourself several hours a day free from electronic devices. No phone, Internet, TV, etc. Make important calls late in the day.

_____ Exercise. Take a walk or a hike. Ride a bike. Row a boat. Don't overdo it; just get the blood flowing and the body moving.

_____ What activities or hobbies help you relax? If you're able to work some of them into your time away (during breaks or at the end of the day), do it. Just don't turn your spiritual/

life-focus retreat into a fishing trip! (Although that is a spiritual experience for some of us guys!)

Answer this question at the end of your retreat: During your time away, what did you do that helped you relax and how/where could you work it into your daily/weekly schedule?

Recharge

This whole experience should help you refocus and recharge, but here are a couple of practical tips:

- ✓ Get some sleep, dude! Some guys think it's a badge of honor to run on little sleep. But experts say we should get at least six hours of sleep per night to stay healthy.
- ✓ Eat healthy! If you decide to fast and pray that will definitely impact the amount of food you eat. (See next section.) But whether you choose to fast or not, drink more water (and less soda) and bring more fruit and veggies (and less junk food). Invest in yourself.

Reconnect...with God

Pray – Prayer is just talking to God like you'd talk to a good friend. You can't have a relationship with someone if you never talk to them. To help you know what to say when you pray, answer the following questions:

- What can you think of to brag on God about and to thank Him for? TIP: Can you see...hear...walk? Do you have a family...a house...a job...food...clothes?

- What questions do you have for God? TIP: Don't be frustrated if God doesn't reveal all the answers in a day or two...give Him some time.
- Is there anything you need to get off your chest? TIP: There's nothing you can say to God that He hasn't already heard... and He knows what you're thinking. So get it out...
- What do you need God to help you with? TIP: You may have more things to write down after you complete the next section: Reevaluate...your priorities.
- TIP: Once-an-hour at the top of the hour stop what you're doing and, using your answers to the questions above, talk to God. You might run out of things to say pretty fast the first time you pray. Don't sweat it. Just keep at it. It will get easier and more natural the more you try.
- TIP: I like to walk while I'm praying and pray out loud. It helps me stay focused (and keeps me from falling asleep).
- TIP: Prayer is talking and *listening*. Pause once in a while after you ask God something. If you get an idea or you think of an answer to something you're praying about, there's a good chance God is speaking to you. *Write it down* and keep praying about it.

Fast (and Pray) – Fasting is prayer on steroids. It's choosing to go without food for a time as you seek God for something really important. You can fast all food, some food (certain foods), or just a meal or two. As you pray throughout the day, every time your body reminds you that you're hungry, it is a reminder to you and to God that you are "hungry for Him" and the direction and answers only He can give. TIP: If you choose to go without food completely, make sure you drink plenty of water and juice to stay hydrated.

Read the Word – Scripture is one of the main ways God speaks to us. If you're not already in some Bible reading plan, I suggest you check out Psalms, Proverbs, or Ecclesiastes in the Old Testament; and

Matthew, Mark, Luke, John, or James in the New Testament. TIP: *Quality* is more important than *quantity*. Read a few verses, then stop and think about what you read and how it applies to your life.

Journal – Journaling isn't for everyone, but it really works for others. Journaling is writing down ideas, thoughts, dreams, etc. that come to you as you pray and read. If you think of something really important, you don't want to forget it! It can also be a great reminder of your spiritual growth as you look back through your notes later in life.

Reevaluate...your priorities

It's easy for our priorities get out of balance. We get so busy that we don't take the time to think about the things that really matter. This section will help you reevaluate your priorities. TIP: You may realize several things in your life that need to change. Don't be overwhelmed. Just focus on improving one thing at a time.

General Fulfillment

Am I happy/fulfilled with my life? _____ YES _____ NO

Why/Why not?

Name one thing you're going to do to move in the direction of being more fulfilled in life:

Relational Health

How healthy are my most important relationships?

	Weak				Average			Really Good		
God:	1	2	3	4	5	6	7	8	9	10
Wife:	1	2	3	4	5	6	7	8	9	10
Kids:	1	2	3	4	5	6	7	8	9	10

If you have more than one child, write their names beside the circled number that represents them

Extended Family

	Weak				Average			Really Good		
Parents:	1	2	3	4	5	6	7	8	9	10

If both of your parents are living, write mom and dad beside the circled number that represents them

	Weak				Average			Really Good		
Sibling(s):	1	2	3	4	5	6	7	8	9	10

If you have more than one sibling, write their names beside the circled number that represents them

	Weak				Average			Really Good		
Friends:	1	2	3	4	5	6	7	8	9	10

If you have more than one friend, write their names beside the circled number that represents them

Name one thing you are going to do to improve your most unhealthy relationships. Examples: ask for forgiveness, spend more time with them, show them more appreciation, go for counseling, etc.

Stewardship of Time and Ability

Am I doing anything to help others (giving of your time/ability)?

_____ YES _____ NO

If YES, what? _____

If NO, why not? _____

Think of someone in need _____ and how you are going to help them _____.
Do it in the next month.

Stewardship of Money

How am I with handling money?

Weak				Average			Really Good		
1	2	3	4	5	6	7	8	9	10

What is my debt load? _____

Do I give to help those in need? _____ YES _____ NO

Do I give to my church?

Tithe (10% of your income) _____ YES _____ NO

Offerings (beyond tithes) _____ YES _____ NO

Do I have any money set aside:

In a Savings Account (how much?) _____

For College Education (how much?)_____

For Life Insurance (how much?) _____

For Retirement (how much?) _____

For Funeral Expenses (how much?) _____

Name one thing you are going to do to improve the way you handle finances:

For some great resources on financial stewardship, check out www.daveramsey.com.

Dreams and Goals

What would you do if you knew you couldn't fail?

Is there anything you've dreamed about doing your whole life?

In Chapter 15 of his book *The Circle Maker,* Mark Batterson shares his life goals. They are excellent. I encourage you to set your own life goals. You only live once! And I encourage you to get a copy of *The Circle Maker.* It's one of the best books on prayer I've ever read.

Recommit...to the things that matter most

God – It all starts with God. When Jesus was asked, "What is the most important commandment?" He replied, *"Love the Lord your God with all your heart and with all your soul, and with all your mind and with all your strength"* (Mark 12:30). In other words, if you make God your highest priority, everything else will fall in place.

To keep God your number one priority long after this retreat ends:

Plan out a daily devotional schedule:

Time: _____   Place: _____

Select a Bible reading plan. YouVersion has some great plans already set up for you. It's available free for your phone, tablet, or computer. Download the app or go to www.bible.com.

Vital Relationships – We all want good relationships. But good relationships take time and attention. Go home recommitted to doing your part. Here are a couple of ideas that could really surprise your family and go a long way toward improving the health of your relationships:

Plan a Date Night with your wife once a month for the next three months:

Date: _____   Idea/Place: _____

Date: _____   Idea/Place: _____

Date: _____   Idea/Place: _____

Who can you call to babysit? (You'll get huge points on this one!)

_____

Plan a weekly Family Night:

Day of the week:

_____ Friday night   _____ Saturday night   _____ Sunday night

Ideas: movie night, pizza night, bowling, game night (then just rotate through them)

Other ideas:

ENDNOTES

Preface

[1]   1 Samuel 30:6b.

Introduction

[1]   1 Chronicles 12:8,22.

[2]   See 1 Samuel 17:28.

[3]   Bear Grylls is best known for his television series "Man vs. Wild" that aired for five years on the Discovery Channel and featured Grylls being dropped into inhospitable places, showing viewers how to survive.

[4]   "Deadliest Warrior," which used to be one of my two son's favorite shows, was on SPIKE TV. Information on historical or modern warriors and their weapons was used to determine which was the deadliest based on tests performed during each episode.

[5]   A shooting competition that airs on the History Channel featuring sixteen contestants, split into two teams of eight, competing in various types of shooting challenges. One by one, the contestants are eliminated until only one remains. That contestant receives a $100,000 grand prize and the title Top Shot.

[6]   See 1 Samuel 16:12.

[7]   I'm talking about the Psalms, many of which were written by David. David's "greatest hit," the Twenty-third Psalm, is one of the most familiar passages in the Bible, known and memorized by millions of people around the world.

[8]   1 Samuel 16:1b NCV.

[9]   Paraphrase of 1 Samuel 16:12.

Chapter 1

[1]   The first time we see this description is in 1 Samuel 13:14. It is repeated in the New Testament in Acts 13:22 *(emphasis mine)*.

[2]   It's important to understand that David didn't try to be the best at *everything*. No one can be the *best* at everything. David understood the

things he was naturally good at and committed himself to becoming the best at them rather than distracting himself with other things.

3   See 1 Samuel 17.
4   See 1 Samuel 10:23.
5   1 Samuel 17:11 MSG *(emphasis mine)*.
6   See 1 Samuel 17:4-7 MSG.
7   See 1 Samuel 17:17-19.
8   1 Samuel 17:26b.
9   1 Samuel 17:40-51 (paraphrased and embellished for extra effect).
10 David waited more than twelve difficult years after his anointing before he actually became king at the age of thirty. See 2 Samuel 5:4.
11 To read more, see 1 Samuel 18 through 2 Samuel 5.
12 1 Samuel 18:7.
13 1 Samuel 18:8-9.
14 See 1 Samuel 24,26.
15 1 Samuel 24:5-7 and 1 Samuel 26:9-11.
16 1 Samuel 22:2 ERV.
17 1 Chronicles 12:22.
18 See John 1:1-14; the "Word" is referring to Jesus Christ.
19 Matthew 14:13; Mark 1:35; Luke 4:42; John 5:19,30.
20 John 3:16-17.
21 See John 15:13 and 1 John 3:8.
22 Hebrews 4:15.
23 2 Thessalonians 2:13 ERV.
24 2 Thessalonians 2:13 MSG.
25 John 3:3, 3:18 and John 14:6 are three of many verses that clearly identify a relationship with Jesus as the key to eternal life.
26 See Matthew 4:18-22 and Mark 1:14-19.

Chapter 2

1   "Hall of Fame" Words and Music by Danny O'Donoghue, Mark Sheehan, James Barry, Andrew Frampton and Will Adams
Copyright (c) 2012 by Universal Music - Z Songs, BMG Sapphire Songs, I Am Composing LLC and Mad Music Publishing
All Rights for BMG Sapphire Songs and I Am Composing LLC Administered by BMG Rights Management (US) LLC
International Copyright Secured All Rights Reserved
Reprinted by Permission of Hal Leonard Corporation
2   Total members of the Hall of Fame as of 2013.

3   The other 29 members of the Pro Football Hall of Fame are coaches, owners, etc.

4   1 Samuel 22:2 ERV.

5   Proverbs 22:1.

6   Genesis 25:21-26.

7   See Acts 7:54-60.

8   See Acts 9.

9   See Acts 9:15.

10 Fasting is choosing to go without food for a meal or a day or several days as you pray and seek God's direction for something really important or hard in your life. Every time your stomach growls, pray something like this, "God, I'm hungry...but I'm more desperate to hear from You and experience a spiritual breakthrough than I am to eat."

11 Proverbs 22:1 ERV.

12 Two of my favorites written by Mark are *In a Pit with a Lion on a Snowy Day* (which is actually based on one of David's Mighty Men, Benaiah) and *The Circle Maker* (one of the best books on prayer I've ever read).

13 Check out Hebrews chapter 11 for a list of the Bible's Hall of Faith.

14 Matthew 25:21,23.

15 Hebrews 4:15.

Chapter 3

1   Population of Meade, Kansas, found at City-Data.com.

2   For information on the Dalton Gang Hideout,
    visit: www.oldmeadecounty.com/hideout.htm; accessed 8/18/14.

3   The Great Plains Field Station was established by the Department of Agriculture to experiment and discover which crops would grow best in the northwest Oklahoma environment.

4   One time I literally escaped from a guy who was chasing us for throwing snowballs at his pickup truck by hiding in the Underground Escape!

5   Looking back, we were lucky we were never greeted by a skunk or some other animal that decided to move into our Underground Escape!

6   Once when my family was on vacation in Iowa, we found my great-grandpa's old deserted cabin, and in it, several rusty metal traps he used to catch fur-bearing animals along the Skunk River. I took some home for souvenirs, and snuck a couple down to the Field Station to see if they still worked. They did...

7   Fatheads are huge, oversized removable decals of pro athletes, football helmets, etc. that can be hung on walls.

8   Thompson Chain Reference Bible Archaeological Supplement. To see pictures of David's hideout, Google Pics of the Bible Cave of Adullam.

Chapter 4

1   Wolverine and the X-Men are part of the "Marvel Universe" created by Stan Lee. Wolverine went from the pages of comic books to the big screen when actor Hugh Jackman brought the tough-talking mutant with indestructible "adamantium claws" to life for a whole new generation.

2   To read some of the challenges and requirements for becoming a Navy Seal, go to http://www.wikihow.com/Become-a-Navy-SEAL. There is also a great survival series on the Discovery Channel called "Dude, You're Screwed!" where five survival experts with different backgrounds (Green Beret, former Navy SEAL, etc.) are kidnapped, blindfolded, and then dropped into one of the world's harshest environments. They each must make their way back to civilization within 100 hours as the four other contestants watch and comment on their progress from a remote command center. It's *crazy!*

3   See 2 Samuel 23:8-12 and 1 Chronicles 11:11-14.

4   See 2 Samuel 23:13-17 and 1 Chronicles 11:15-19.

5   See 2 Samuel 23:18-19 and 1 Chronicles 11:20-21.

6   See 2 Samuel 23:20-23 and 1 Chronicles 11:22-25.

7   See 1 Chronicles 11:2,14.

8   Ephesians 4:7 The Living Bible.

9   Ephesians 2:10 The Living Bible.

10   Rick Warren, *What On Earth Am I Here For?* (Grand Rapids, MI: Zondervan, 2004), 225.

11   John 10:10 NLT.

12   See 2 Corinthians 2:11 NLT.

13   2 Corinthians 10:12 God's Word Translation.

14   James 4:14.

15   Moses, one of the greatest leaders in the Bible, argued with God because he felt unqualified to represent God before Pharaoh. See Genesis 3:11 and Genesis 4:10-13.

16   See 2 Corinthians 12:7-10.

17   See Isaiah 6:1-8.

Chapter 5

[1] *King Arthur;* released July 7, 2004, by Touchstone Pictures and Jerry Bruckheimer Films.

[2] *Braveheart;* released May 24, 1995, by Paramount Pictures and 20th Century Fox.

[3] John 10:10 NLT.

[4] See Ezekiel 22:23-29.

[5] Ezekiel 22:30.

[6] Psalm 27:1b MSG.

Chapter 6

[1] Proverbs 27:6.

[2] Proverbs 27:17 NLT.

[3] See 1 Chronicles 12:16-18.

[4] My paraphrase of 1 Chronicles 12:18.

[5] 2 Samuel 23:15 or 1 Chronicles 11:17.

[6] The Hulk is the alter-ego of Dr. Bruce Banner. After being exposed to a high dose of gamma radiation, Dr. Banner's DNA was altered. Whenever he gets angry, Banner transforms into a giant, indestructible, muscular green monster.

[7] See James 2:23 and 2 Chronicles 20:7.

[8] Exodus 33:11 Good News Translation (GNT).

[9] Psalm 8:4 ERV.

[10] John 15:15 ERV.

[11] Psalm 119:160 ERV.

[12] Hebrews 13:5 GNT.

[13] Matthew 28:20 ERV.

[14] John 15:13 NCV.

Chapter 7

[1] See 2 Samuel 23:39 and 1 Chronicles 11:41.

[2] See 2 Samuel 11:6-17.

[3] Galatians 5:17 NLT.

[4] Some other ways God talks to us is through preaching and teaching, through other believers, and by way of the Holy Spirit guiding us.

[5] 2 Peter 1:21 says of Scripture and the prophecies written in the Bible that the prophets did not think these things up on their own, but they were guided by the Spirit of God. And 2 Timothy 3:16 (NLT) says, *"All Scripture is inspired by God..."*

6   Hebrews 4:12 ERV.

7   Galatians 5:22-23 gives a list of the good character traits that God begins
        to develop in us when we regularly feed the fire of the Spirit.

8   Galatians 5:17 NLT.

9   Men literally have a couple of seconds to make the right choice about
        sexual thoughts and images. The longer you wait, the hotter the flame
        is going to get and the harder it will be to put it out. So make quick
        decisions!

10   Galatians 5:19-21 gives a list of sins that can take over our lives when we
        regularly feed the fire of the flesh.

11   Galatians 5:16 NCV.

12   Mark is a fictitious name but the situation was real.

13   Matthew 7:12 NCV.

14   Hebrews 11:25.

15   Numbers 32:23 MSG.

16   2 Samuel 11:15 Contemporary English Version.

17   Luke 12:3 New International Reader's Version.

18   2 Samuel 11:1 (Good News Translation).

19   Psalm 51:17 NCV.

20   Psalm 51:4 ERV.

21   Psalm 51:3 ERV, NIV.

22   One example is Matthew 5:23-24 (MSG) where Jesus said, *"If you enter
        your place of worship and are about to make an offering and you suddenly
        remember a grudge a friend has against you...leave immediately, go to this
        friend and make things right. Then and only then, come back and work
        things out with God."*

23   2 Samuel 12:13.

24   1 John 1:9 CEV.

25   Numbers 32:23 MSG.

Chapter 8

1   To read more details about David's time living among the Philistines,
        check out 1 Samuel 27 and 29.

2   1 Samuel 30:3 ERV.

3   1 Samuel 30:4 ERV.

4   1 Samuel 30:6a CEV.

5   1 Samuel 30:6b NLT.

6   1 Samuel 30:8.

7   1 Samuel 30:8 ERV.

[8]   1 Samuel 30:9-10.

[9]   1 Samuel 30:17-18.

[10] My revision of John 15:13.

[11] Ephesians 6:10-13 ERV.

[12] 1 Samuel 30:17-18.

Chapter 9

[1]   See 2 Samuel 23:11-12.

[2]   See 2 Samuel 23:9-10 and 1 Chronicles 11:12-14.

[3]   See 2 Samuel 23:8.

[4]   See 1 Chronicles 11:11.

[5]   See 2 Samuel 23:13-17 and 1 Chronicles 11:15-19.

[6]   See 2 Samuel 23:18-19 and 1 Chronicles 11:20-21.

[7]   See 2 Samuel 23:20-23 and 1 Chronicles 11:22-25.

[8]   1 Chronicles 12:22.

[9]   Psalm 107:2 NIV.

[10] Psalm 144:3-4 MSG.

[11] John 10:10b MSG.

Appendix A

[1]   Romans 3:23 NLT.

[2]   There are many great books that teach the basics of following Christ. One I've used is *Follow* by Dan McNaughton and Bryan Koch. It teaches the seven main steps to becoming a fully devoted follower of Jesus, complete with interactive questions in each chapter and Leader's Notes in the back.

[3]   Matthew 28:19-20 is known as The Great Commission: "*…go and make disciples of all nations, baptizing them in the name of the Father and of the Son and of the Holy Spirit, and teaching them to obey everything I have commanded you.*"

ABOUT THE AUTHOR

Wayde Wilson has been a pastor for 29 years. He graduated from Evangel University with a degree in communications and is ordained with the Assemblies of God.

Wayde is an avid outdoorsman who enjoys watching sports and spending time with friends. He and his wife, Sonya, have three children: daughter Tristin, and her husband Jimmy; son Trevor and his wife Kayla; and son, Travis.

Although he celebrates every life changed by Christ, Wayde particularly loves challenging men to be spiritually courageous leaders.

Contact Information

For more information about Wayde's ministry,
visit www.waydewilson.com.
Follow Wayde on Twitter @WaydeWWilson
or Facebook @Wayde-Sonya Wilson

FORM YOUR OWN CIRCLE OF SWORDS!

Circle of Swords

Small Group Leader's Guide

Wayde Wilson

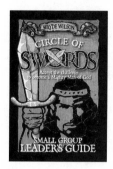

Leader's Guide Includes:

- Suggested Ground Rules for your group
- Additional questions and discussion starters
- Weekly Sharpen your Sword memory verse
- Downloadable pdf format allows you to print individual pages

To purchase the Circle of Swords Small Group Leader's Guide, visit www.waydewilson.com